AN IMPERIAL AFFAIR

AN IMPERIAL AFFAIR

Portrait of an Australian Marriage

JOHN RICKARD

MONASH University Publishing

Monash University Publishing
Building 4, Monash University
Clayton, Victoria 3800, Australia
www.publishing.monash.edu

Monash University Publishing brings to the world publications which advance the best traditions of humane and enlightened thought.

Monash University Publishing titles pass through a rigorous process of independent peer review.

http://publishing.monash.edu/books/ia-9781922235275.html

Series: Biography

Design: Les Thomas

National Library of Australia Cataloguing-in-Publication entry:

Author: Rickard, John, 1935- , author.

Title: An imperial affair : portrait of an Australian marriage / John Rickard.

ISBN: 9781922235275 (paperback)

Subjects: Rickard, Philip--Marriage; Rickard, Pearl--Marriage; Rickard, John, 1935- ;
   Authors--Family relationships--Australia--Biography; Marriage--Social
   aspects--Australia; Families--Social aspects--Australia; Social values--
   Australia; Australia--Social life and customs--1901-1945.

Dewey Number: 994.041

Printed in Australia by Griffin Press an Accredited ISO AS/NZS 14001:2004 Environmental Management System printer.

CONTENTS

Contents

PREFACE

Introducing his Viennese family saga, *Good Living Street*, Tim Bonyhady remarks that 'while it is in the nature of parents to want and get the last word in arguments when their children are young, it is a prerogative of the living to have the last word about the dead'. True enough, though I am uncomfortable with the implication that there is an element of getting even with them involved. There is a sense, however, in which 'the last word' is never said: 'the living' may not necessarily agree among themselves.

My parents died a long time ago, yet they are still with me. We often regret the questions we didn't ask of our parents when they were alive, but I suspect that at the time we are restrained by a sense of boundaries that it would be impolite, or even painful, to cross. It was only when, years later, my father's wartime letters to my mother came to my attention that I began to feel the need, if only for my own sake, to unravel their story.

I am indebted to my sister, Barbara Fisher, who has allowed me to draw upon her eloquent poems, taken principally from her collection *Still Life, Other Life*, described by Elizabeth Webby as showing 'her mastery of the compressed narrative that is poetry at its best'. While we share memories of our family, we inevitably have different perspectives, particularly from the time when the family unit was beginning to disperse. Barbara has supported the project from the beginning and read my drafts, and our conversations have contributed to the memoir presented here.

The family correspondence, diaries and documents I have drawn upon are largely in my possession. Archival material included the usual genealogical sources (births, marriages and deaths) both here and in England, and my father's RAAF service record. I also spent a day familiarizing myself with Andover in Hampshire, and in London, armed with my camera, I walked the streets of the Kensington area that my parents knew well. The photographs and paintings are held either by Barbara or myself.

I am very appreciative of the critical help and support of my friends of the life writing group in Melbourne: Ian Britain, Barbara Caine, Susan Foley, Ruth Ford, Jim Hammerton, Katie Holmes, Jim Mitchell, Chips Sowerwine, Al Thomson and Christina Twomey. They came on this journey with me, chapter by chapter, reading my self-conscious drafts. For their advice and suggestions I thank Bain Attwood, David Chandler,

Bill Grundy, Peter Hocker, Phillipa McGuinness, Brenda Niall, Terry Owen, Ron Porter, Sam Spiers and Pauline Woodward.

I am extremely grateful for Monash University Publishing taking on *An Imperial Affair* and I thank Nathan Hollier in particular for his interest and encouragement, and also Les Thomas, Sarah Cannon and Kate Hatch for their contribution.

In the end, of course, it is my memoir and my responsibility. But I am confident that, in the sense that my parents are still with me, this memoir is not the last word.

PROLOGUE

It begins with a shoebox of letters. They are letters from my father, Philip, to my mother, Pearl, written from London during the Second World War. My sister has passed them onto me: I don't think I have seen them before. My mother, who had kept them in this David Jones shoebox, died in 1962. After that my father must have kept them and, following his death in 1977, my stepmother likewise. And now the shoebox is in my hands, and I start to read them with a mixture of voyeuristic curiosity and a certain shyness about invading the privacy of their world.

There are over a hundred of them, carefully numbered, so that if a letter went astray or went down with a ship its loss would be known. My father was an officer in the RAAF, in stores and equipment, and was stationed in London from mid-1941 to early 1943. The letters tell an interesting story of what life was like in England after the blitz, when the immediate threat of invasion seemed to have passed, but when it was still difficult to imagine an end to the conflict that saw most of Europe in German hands.

But there is another story buried here, the story of my parents' marriage. It is, at first appearances at least, a one-sided story, as my mother's letters from Australia do not survive. This was their first long separation, and it was not easy to sustain the dialogue between husband and wife across the seas when a letter might take months to reach its destination.

I dip into the letters, penned in my father's firm, well-ordered handwriting. I hear his voice, recognisable at times, but at other times almost the voice of a stranger. And I am trying to imagine what lies behind the words, what is not being said in these loving and informative letters to my mother.

And then I find a clue. Between two letters a small piece of folded pale yellow paper. I open it to find a tiny snapshot of an attractive, dark-haired woman in a summer dress, seated in a garden, a small child by her side. On the paper is written, *in my mother's handwriting*: 'Mrs Clare Moilliet, Lime Court, Linden Gardens, London. W.2.'

So this is Clare. I have always known about her, but have not seen a photograph of her before. Nor did I know her full name. She was just Clare, the mysterious Clare. Clare was the Other Woman.

Reading her name on this slip of paper the years melt away and I am taken back to when I first heard it. I am tucked up in my bed in the sleep-out in our Dubbo house during the War. The sleep-out, open to the weather like a verandah, is attached to the master bedroom. It is a quiet night outside so the canvas blinds are not flapping as they do when it's wet and windy. I have been awakened by voices in the stillness of the dark.

Lying in bed, my parents are arguing. Earlier in the evening, over the washing up in the kitchen, there had been a tearful 'scene' and this middle-of-the-night conversation is the aftermath. I visualise them in the double bed, lying on their backs, speaking into the air, their bodies not touching.

These sad, ghostly voices seep into my mind. I lie huddled in my bed, still and silent, afraid to move, listening. My mother accusingly mentions the name 'Clare' which lodges in my memory. Somehow my mother has found out about Clare. Father is not saying much, almost as if, unusually for him, he is at a loss for words.

My mother utters the word 'divorce'. I do not really understand what that means, but I know from the way that she says it that 'divorce' is something ugly and terrible, but perhaps something I will have to learn to live with.

I only wish they would please stop talking like this, but my mother's voice, full of pain and resentment, goes on, my father helplessly unable to say anything to placate her.

But I do drift off to sleep. In the morning what I have heard in the night takes on the feeling of a nightmare. Except that I know it is real.

It may not have been her intention, but Clare almost brought my parents' marriage to an end. For this was no ordinary wartime dalliance. Even when, after a brief separation, my parents negotiated a reconciliation, Clare did not go away. She was still there, just as she is now, in the photograph in my hand.

How had my mother acquired this photograph and why, I wonder, had she kept it and so carefully, dispassionately, recorded Clare's full name and address? She had kept Father's letters when, having learnt of the affair, she might have been tempted to destroy them. But by slipping this piece of paper with the photograph in amongst the letters it is as if she is saying, *this is what these letters are not telling you.* And here is the documentary evidence. Clare was, it informs us, also married, and, indeed, the mother of the little girl who commands her attention in the photograph.

This is the story of my parent's marriage. But I want it to be about Philip and Pearl, not just about my father and my mother. It is the lot of sons and daughters not to know our parents when they are young. Here I shall try to imagine the story as they lived and experienced it.

Their story is bound up with the larger story of Australia's role as a 'dominion' in the British Empire, which, although it had entered a terminal decline, still commanded the cultural allegiance of most Australians. My parents, like most middle-class folk then, took England and Empire as a given.

Philip and Pearl's marriage was born of a different world to ours. Marriage itself was different then: couples entered it expecting it to be 'till death do us part': for my mother to raise the possibility of divorce was shocking, because in those days it was associated with the sleazy and humiliating sensationalism of courtroom proceedings. Australia was a much smaller and more conformist society, with a population of a mere seven million, and although the War had exposed the irrelevance of Britain to our defence, the imperial connection remained fundamental to our sense of national identity. This was also the world I grew up in: I inherited its values, even if later I was to grow out of them. I was, as it turned out, if not a rebel, at least a dissident voice.

But I am still the child in the sleep-out bed, an occasional witness to their drama, who, glimpsing this adult mystery of love and betrayal, wants to find out what it was really all about.

Chapter 1

SYDNEY: COURTSHIP

When my father went a-courting
he brought my mother fruit,
fresh nectarines in a basket
and wore his Sunday suit.

Picked them in the garden
and walked across the hill
quickly to determine
if she could love him still.

I think that ardent summer
began the fabled time
when all fruit was much finer
but nectarines were sublime.

Mulberries then had flavour
and peaches knew no pest,
figs were fat and fleshy
but nectarines were best.

Muscatels were sweeter then
and so were mandarines
but none are so remembered
as those fresh nectarines.

I never saw the family tree
that bore these gifts of love,
nor tasted of its famous fruit
this legend to disprove.

Yet hearing of the nectarines
I know that they were sweet,
for when the time was summoned
the years fell at their feet.

— Barbara Fisher

It was a Sunday afternoon when Philip climbed the hill bearing his gift of summer nectarines. He had been playing the organ at church in the morning; Pearl had been in the choir. Music had brought them together. It was 1924 when, in the old-fashioned, respectable sense, they became lovers, but they were not formally engaged until Christmas 1925; long courtships were common then, and it was almost another two years before they were married at St Anne's, in the Sydney suburb of Ryde, which still had the feeling of being on the edge of countryside. It became part of the family mythology that Philip nominated 31 September 1927 as the preferred date for the wedding, only to be told by the rector of St Anne's that not even love had the power to change the Gregorian calendar. He was right not only about the calendar, but in recognising that Philip and Pearl were very much in love.

Philip Rickard was the youngest of seven children and his mother's favourite. The Rickards were a respectable, church-going family, well known in the St Anne's parish. Philip's father, William, was an accountant, and in a postcard photograph presents as a solid, unimaginative-looking man, gazing implacably into the middle distance. His wife, Victoria, whose name was inspired by her sharing a birthday with the Queen, was straight-backed and perhaps strait-laced, but bright-eyed and with the hint of a smile in the photograph as she confronts the camera direct. In 1907 they had built a house, 'Vicuna', in Ryde, which was then an outer suburb, largely through an inheritance of Victoria's.

They seemed happy enough as a family, but as with most large families of that generation there were visitations of tragedy. Just a few weeks after the outbreak of the Great War in August 1914 their twenty-year old daughter, Ruth, together with a friend, died in a drowning accident. The St Anne's paper called it 'a stunning tragedy': 'On the threshold of womanhood, the door into the Future was opened from within – they passed through – and it has closed behind them.' It was difficult to disguise the pointlessness of such a death.

Philip, who had just turned twelve when war broke out, had three elder brothers – Jonathan (Jack), Thomas (Tom) and William (Bill) – and as loyal Anglo-Australians it wasn't long before they enlisted. One year later the three brothers were farewelled at a church social. Jack had been an important figure in the parish as superintendent of the Sunday School, a member of the choir and the church committee as well as a synod representative. He was presented with a pocket compass and a fountain pen. Tom, a chorister and Sunday School teacher, and Bill, the youngest of the trio and a chorister, were given wrist watches, something of a novelty for men at this time. The fob watch had been part of the masculine image; wrist watches had been principally for women, but during the War it came to be appreciated that on the battlefield the wrist watch had many advantages.

The same issue of the *Ryde Church Paper* was reporting 'the roll of honour' from Gallipoli: although they were to serve on the Western Front they had some idea of the kind of war ahead of them. On their attestation paper forms they describe themselves as 'British born', although all had been born in Sydney. They were, of course, as all Australians were at this time, British subjects, and for the form they were filling in 'Australian born' was not even an option. And the war itself was, as far as Australia was concerned, a British war in defence of empire.

To see three of their sons going off to the trenches of France was bad enough for William and Victoria (who in the family was usually known as Tottie), but William worked for a German shipping company and lost his job with the closing down of its Australian operations. He was in his late fifties and was never to work again. It was now up to the sons, even while at war, to support their parents.

Jack and Tom, as mature young middle-class men, 32 and 26 respectively, were soon commissioned as officers; Bill, 23, whose occupation was given as electrical engineer, did not appear to aspire to such a role and became a bombardier, rising to the rank of fitter corporal. Jack was wounded and hospitalised in England not long before the Armistice, while the war left Bill with a legacy of partial deafness.

They were, however, fortunate to survive that terrible war. Tom was the unlucky one. On 19 July 1916 he led his men over the top in the charge of the Battle of Fromelles and was struck down in No-Man's-Land about 150 yards from the Australian trench. His left arm was shattered at the shoulder. It seems that he was so badly wounded that, even if it had been possible to bring him back in, he would not have survived. Sadly, in the confusion of the aftermath of this horrific battle in which so many were killed, the family were given some hope that he might have been rescued and transferred to a hospital in England. It was another year before a court of inquiry officially recorded his death. Under 'Place of Burial' the form noted 'Particulars not yet to hand'. The particulars were never to hand.

While his brothers were at war Philip was fast growing up. On 27 October 1918 he penned a letter to Jack in England. He was eager to impress on his eldest brother that he was no longer a boy but had entered the portals of manhood. It is a letter brimming over with youthful confidence, written in a mature, business-like hand. He opens on a serious note, reporting on a sermon by the rector at a service marking the anniversary of St Columb's, a branch church of St Anne's:

> The Rector preached an extremely vigorous sermon concerning the likelihood of children becoming lost to their homes, parents, religion and specially morality. He was very plain and candid, making no nice distinctions.

Then to the weather: 'This day a fearful hurricane has been raging, laden with dust and sweeping all before it.' There had also been a bushfire nearby, but, bushfire and hurricane notwithstanding, he had spent part of the afternoon 'playing over some of the church music'.

But all this is a prelude to the most important news, a significant rite of passage:

> I am wondering what you will say when I tell you I entered long'uns to day. I started shaving last Sunday. Mother says it makes me look taller than ever. I feel quite set up in my new suit and tall stiff collar. As for shaving, I have only done so twice, and yet feel an expert at it. I received numerous and sundry congratulations and compliments. I shall try and get a snap taken to send to you.

Reminding Jack of Sunday School affairs he is delighted to report that the annual picnic, always a great event in the church calendar and this year at Meadow Bank Park, 'is hoving in sight', and that he has been placed on a committee to organise the races and games. 'Given a fine day, and a calm river, it promises to be a glorious time.'

Philip was in his penultimate year at Sydney High School, where he had just been placed on the Tuck Shop Committee. 'We manage the biz for the benefit of the School Sports Union. It is a cosy little place just inside the big school arch with its iron gate'. And it had the virtue of giving him 'a little experience in bills and money matters'. He had also helped organise the school's annual mock banquet, where he praises the speeches made by boys who were leaving ('clear, decisive, energetic and sensible'). One prefect spoke of 'the vulgar, and ungentlemanly conduct of the other high schools' in games: 'Fort St., North Sydney etc. are absolutely rotten sports, they cheat right and left.' As the only high school that was also a 'Great Public School' (competing with the leading private schools) it was a cut above its lowlier brethren.

Only in the final paragraph does Philip bring the letter round to the family's concern for Jack:

> First thoughts on hearing of your wound were of regret, but later of thankfulness that you were spared. The news from base, and also your cablegram saying you were in Wandsworth Hospital removed great doubt and anxiety from our minds. Many kind friends have asked after you.

By the time Jack received this letter the war would have been over. The world of Sunday school picnics and tuck shops must have seemed a far cry from the inferno he, along with Tom and Bill, had encountered in the trenches of France; yet perhaps it was reassuring to know that distant, innocent world was still there. Certainly he would have been amused by the gentlemanly swagger acquired by the boy they had left behind three years ago. He kept the letter, which their mother, Tottie, was to put aside as a family memento. It now resides in my grandmother's writing box, along with a sparse selection of family documents, which has ended up in my hands.

Philip did well at school and won the approbation of his teachers. The headmaster spoke very highly of 'his character and general conduct'. His

English teacher, while noting that young Philip could 'express himself very clearly and forcibly', praised his 'public spirit' and 'his affectionate, interesting disposition'. 'Affectionate' is not a word one would expect to find in a reference from a teacher, but it perhaps says something about his warmth and enthusiasm, which made him popular with both masters and boys.

While undertaking his Economics degree he got a job in the Probate Office at the Supreme Court, first as a clerk and later as cashier. It was his aim to qualify as an accountant, like his father. It was a secure, if humdrum job, but security was a major family consideration, particularly given his father's fate with the German shipping company.

Six foot tall, dark-haired with strong features, he faced the world with a certain restless energy. The youth who had been praised for his 'public spirit' and 'affectionate, interesting disposition' longed for something more engaging and exciting than the Probate Office. In the meantime music – and the emotional grandeur of the organ in particular – captivated and absorbed him and was capable of blocking out the daily tedium of office work.

The Rickards' circumstances suffered with William being thrown out of work during the War (though there were those who thought he had been less than persevering in the search for new employment) but the family at least had the secure base of 'Vicuna', thanks to Tottie's modest inheritance. Pearl's family, on the other hand, had had a much tougher time.

Pearl was the fifth of ten children. Her mother, Edith Tunks, could claim to be a first-fleeter; William Tunks, her great grandfather, was a marine on the fleet flagship, HMS *Sirius*. However, this was a time when not much was made of this kind of heritage, particularly as in this case it was linked to the family's historic embarrassment, Sarah Lyons, the feisty convict whom William had met on Norfolk Island and with whom he was to share his life, together bringing up their children, including Edith's grandfather. To make matters worse, William and Sarah, like many of the convict generation, had never bothered to get married. As a result in Samuel Marsden's notorious female convict muster of 1806 she was listed as a concubine. The family's convict heritage became a dark family secret, and I grew up not knowing anything about my convict ancestor Sarah.

When Edith married William Quarterman Bragg at St Peter's church, Woolloomooloo, in 1895 she might have had expectations of a secure family life. The Braggs seemed a solid middle-class clan; indeed William's father was part-owner of a Lithgow coal mine. William, the eldest son, named after his father, described his occupation as 'mining accountant', so clearly the mine was a point of reference for the wider family. At the time of Pearl's birth in 1903 he was working for the Coal Association.

There was, however, the suggestion of a shadow over the marriage from the start. William and Edith's first child, Maud, was born seven months after the wedding. Some eyebrows might have been raised and lips pursed. Certainly for Edith marriage meant an immediate introduction to almost twenty years of pregnancies, the children arriving at regular two yearly intervals. This, of course, was still the expectation of many women: at least Edith survived the ten births, and none of their offspring died in childhood. But William was a gambler, and, it seemed, mentally unstable, and this affected the family's financial viability. They were not, like the Rickards, homeowners, and during these years there were several moves.

My mother was born into a family of four small children, the eldest Maud aged seven. And as she grew up five more boys were added to the tumultuous household. The senior children, particularly Maud and Will, the eldest son, soon acquired responsibilities for helping care for the new arrivals. (Indeed Maud, who took a certain calm satisfaction in exercising authority, came to be much feared by the youngest of the brood.) In large families children usually form particular ties from amongst their number: of all her brothers Pearl was closest to Jim, just two years her junior, whom she tended to take under her wing.

Young Will, of course, inevitably bore his father's name, but most of the children were not overburdened with family names. Pearl Mildred Henrietta Bragg was an exception. 'Pearl' came from the youngest of her father's siblings; 'Mildred' after her mother's youngest sister; and "Henrietta' after her maternal grandmother. My mother never liked her first name, but, as far as the family was concerned, she was stuck with it.

It was not a particularly happy childhood, as their father's behaviour grew more erratic and, at times, violent. Pearl also fell victim to rheumatic fever. She recovered but it left its mark on her. And then in 1912 came the crisis from which the family was never to recover. It is not clear exactly what happened, but something snapped in William's mind; he ran amok in some way sufficient for him to be 'put away', as the term went, in a mental asylum. In this crisis his brother James (known to the family as Uncle Jim) took charge and must have organised the committal, with Edith's consent. Edith was pregnant at the time with the last of her ten children.

The household of Ethel Turner's *Seven Little Australians* (1894) is portrayed as delightfully chaotic, but one needs to be reminded that their situation was one of comparative affluence, with servants providing a comfortable buffer. Edith, faced with bringing up ten little Australians on her own, was sentenced to the life of the shabby-genteel. Uncle Jim organised some grudging Bragg family financial support, but the children were expected to soon take over the responsibility of supporting their mother. The family had to bear the shame of having a father who was deemed insane.

Young Will worked as a storeman. Unlike the Rickards this was not a family where anyone entertained thoughts of higher education. When the Great War broke out in 1914 it was not surprising that he should give some thought to joining the 'six bob a day tourists', as the first volunteers were dubbed, but he was still to turn seventeen. But this did not exempt Will, a skinny youth (5'10" and 130lbs according to his enlistment form) from being handed a white feather by a young woman who no doubt thought she was doing her bit for the war effort. In January 1916 he put his age forward a month or two and enlisted.

With the heavy toll of casualties from the disastrous Gallipoli campaign now public knowledge, Will, like the Rickard brothers, must have had some idea what he was letting himself in for. His letters home reveal a stoical young man, dourly aware of his family responsibilities. 'Don't forget to let me know what Uncle Jim is doing about Father's affairs' he writes in one of his first letters home to his mother. He several times expresses concern that she is getting the designated portion of his pay. Like most Australians he is not into flagwaving, but is 'longing to get a cut at the Germans'. He makes a point of sending postcards to the two youngest children, Jack and Ray, and acknowledges a letter from 'Pearlie'. As well as the regular letters to his mother he writes occasionally to his father though without any expectation of getting a reply. He spends Christmas and New Year in the trenches, his first experience of the firing line, and reports that 'I did not feel nearly so nervous under fire as I thought I would, in fact I supprised [sic] myself'. He was a machine gunner and in one letter gives vent to a surge of blood lust, almost as if it's a relief from the muddy boredom of life in the trenches: 'the first shot we fired we hit a hun and he yelled and squealed like a stuck pig'.

These letters were no doubt read to the family, though perhaps Pearl and the younger children were spared the killing. But in 1917 the letters falter. He struggled to find 'news' to tell them; or at least the only news was the daily toll of death and destruction, made worse by winter and darkness. It was as if the war had numbed him. 'I feel quite ashamed of myself', he confesses, apologising for the long gaps between letters.

At the same time he is still concerned about how the family at home is faring. They had recently been forced to move house – the reason for this unwelcome uprooting is not clear. Could they have been behind with the rent? 'I know you have a hard time of it trying to battle along on what little you have,' he writes in his last letter, adding that she was not to worry about putting aside any of his pay for him for his return. It was a sign of the family's stringent circumstances that Edith was never in a position to send parcels to Will: the few that he received came from an aunt.

At about this time the large framed photograph of Will which had pride of place on the wall suddenly came crashing to the floor, shattering the glass. When news came that he was wounded, and, subsequently, killed in action, this dramatic incident was seen as a portent. His body was never recovered. So another young life had been snuffed out in faraway France. It is a pity that news of his death could not be conveyed to the woman who presented him with the white feather.

Coming so soon after the incarceration of William it cast a pall over the household. Quite apart from the personal tragedy of his death, it also meant cutting off one source of income for the survival of the family back in Sydney. Pearl had just turned thirteen when Will's death was confirmed. These growing up years were made more difficult by the separation from her elder sister Sybil who, in the wake of William's expulsion from the household, was farmed out to rich relatives. Sybil was attractive and personable, and something of a favourite in the wider family; Pearl had been close to Sybil, who had none of Maud's forbidding quality. She missed Sybil, and was probably just a little envious of the much more exciting social life her sister was enjoying.

This was a time when it was becoming more acceptable for young middle-class women to seek paid employment, though it was understood this would cease with marriage. But Pearl does not appear to have taken this opportunity. This may have been because there was still some concern about her health in the wake of her childhood rheumatic fever; possibly, too, as the only daughter living at home – Maud having married and Sybil living with relatives – she was considered more useful in the home.

Sybil's marriage was an important event for Pearl. She was marrying Sidney, an upright, sober young man, a teetotaller in fact. But Pearl's chief memory of that wedding day was her sister in floods of tears as she prepared for the fateful journey down the aisle. At a time when the ideal of marrying for love had been popularised, had she found herself making a choice on much more pragmatic grounds, and now experienced pangs of regret at the life-long commitment she was making? Of course, Syril saw it through and made the best of things.

But perhaps Sybil's wedding day tears left Pearl hoping for something more like the ideal of romantic love. She might have been perceived as a serious young woman; certainly there was an element of reserve. She was hardly a flapper, but she kept up with the swiftly changing fashions of the 1920s. Her shortish straight hair parted in the middle (it would be some years before she risked a permanent wave) gave her face an oval-shaped look; she was not a beauty in the conventional sense, but there was a grace and naturalness about her, and the flash of a smile, fresh and unforced, could light up her face. Music was an outlet: in a family that was not particularly musical both she and Sybil learnt singing, and went on to sing in choirs and as soloists. Music, too, had the power to conjure up a beauty from within.

The music of the church might have brought Philip and Pearl together, but it was not the only music in their lives. A popular song of some significance for them was a languorous, romantic ballad, 'Marchéta', billed rather misleadingly as 'A Love Song of Old Mexico'. Composed by Victor Schertzinger, an American song writer probably best known for 'I Remember You', it dated from 1913, but proved its durability, going on to be recorded by Richard Tauber, Mario Lanza and Nat King Cole, amongst others. Young Philip might have been a loyal Anglo-Australian, but American popular culture, so influential in the new media of cinema and wireless, was seeping into the texture of Australian life.

We do not know how Philip and Pearl encountered this 'love song of Old Mexico', though it was a ballad that might have passed muster at a church social for young people. But it became a kind of talisman for them. It is, the sheet music tells us, to be sung 'dreamily', the singer longing for the return of his Marchéta :

> In dreams I can see you, your sweet face with love all aglow.
> Your voice, like soft music, still echoes around me
> As in the old days long ago.

When Philip presented Pearl in 1924 with a leather-bound 'Autographs' book, it was inscribed to 'My Sweetheart, Dearest Marchéta':

> This little book and all that herein lies
> Was in the first place meant just for your eyes ...

But if she chose to show it to her friends, well, that would be alright too. He signed himself, with a slight confusion of languages, as 'Toujours le Vôtre, Filipo Ricardo'.

Philip wooed Pearl not only with poems but with songs. Indeed, the first poem he wrote in the 'Autographs' book after the dedication was in fact the text of a song, 'Pearls', written for his Marchéta:

> Most precious pearl upon my breast,
> To you alone I have confess'd
> My secret hopes and fears ...
> Emblem of faith serene and pure
> Your perfect beauty will endure,
> Though countless years roll by ...

Remarkably unselfconscious about the romantic context of the song, he showed it to his music teacher who sought an opinion from a colleague. 'A.H.' wrote on the manuscript returned to Philip: 'Should write really well when he knows more about his subject (Harmony etc.)'. It was sufficient encouragement – along with Pearl's delight (after all, how many girls had songs dedicated to them by their lovers?) – to motivate Philip to write a batch of songs during their courtship.

He presented 'Pearls' very formally to 'Miss Pearl M.H. Bragg' on 3 May 1924, not long before her twenty-first birthday. One might imagine it almost reconciled her to her name. He was, of course, regularly accompanying her on the piano and was charmed by her mezzo-soprano voice. He wrote a poem celebrating the experience:

There is no sound that charms me more
Than when you sing to me.
No music wields more subtle power
Than when you sing to me.
Flutes may pipe and cellos sigh
Or organs peel and thunder,
Yet none of these can stir my soul
To such enraptured wonder ...

When seated at the piano playing
Accompanying harmonies
Sometimes I wish they were as soft
As whispering winds in trees.
Sometimes I wish the chords would ring
In echoes loud and long;
Sometimes I only wish to hear
The beauty of your song.

And the intimate relationship between piano and voice, between accompanist and singer, their sounds in dialogue and then mingling, beautifully matches and echoes the relationship between lovers. I cannot remember my father or mother making any reference to these poems and songs, which they probably looked back upon with amused embarrassment. They had more to do with the popular idiom of 'Marchéta' than with the classical music they were being introduced to in their singing and organ lessons. But they were part of their love story.

The courtship came to a head on Boxing Day 1925. After each had had the ritual Christmas Day midday dinner with their families (hot of course, regardless of the weather – roast chicken, if you were lucky, with stuffing, bread sauce and masses of potato and pumpkin, followed by plum pudding, a treasure trove of small silver coins for the children, with gallons of custard) they escaped their homes on Boxing Day for a picnic at Lane Cove. And while Philip rowed the boat along the river, Pearl, with all the unselfconsciousness of someone in love, sang for him, giving him what he later described as 'an impromptu concert' on the water.

It was the perfect moment for the formal proposal, though it is clear there was no doubt about the answer, as Philip came with a ring to present to Pearl:

What shall it mean to us – this diamond ring,
This emblem tradition hath for true loving?
Shall it not mean –

That I will always give you all my love,
Without restraint, entirely trusting you.
That you will always be my ain true love

Whose soft warm kisses thrill me 'thru' and 'thru'.
Shall it not mean that you and I have found
Our hearts are now inseparably bound?

Inseparably bound. There is a photograph of them bathing which may have been taken on this day. They are up to their shoulders in the water, standing close together. His face is in profile, bending a little towards her, with an expression of affectionate solicitude. Pearl, in her white bathing cap, is acknowledging his interest with a shy smile. There is no one else in the picture, the river bank behind them deserted, though Pearl's shyness may reflect an awareness of that one witness to their love, the person wielding the camera.

Their romance now seemed to reach a plateau. It was not that their relationship lost any of its intensity. Poems and songs flowed from Philip's pen. Nor was there any doubt that Pearl was rather swept away by her lover's ardour. She wrote each poem neatly in the book he had given her. Any period of separation, however short, was painful, and in a poem, 'If You Were Here', Philip expressed his wonder at the strength of her love:

And yet compared with yours my love is poor
For yours has all the strength of mine and more.

And in the last poem in the book he paid tribute to the inspiration Pearl gave him, which, while it echoed a traditional notion of feminine moral virtue, bore the stamp of sincerity, particularly in its fusing of the physical and spiritual:

Only she
Can rouse the depths of passionate love in me,
And only she can give me the enobling grace
To seek the highest ideals and live them thru'.

It did seem that for both of them this was their first real experience of such emotional intimacy, there being no family stories or jokes about discarded admirers or girlfriends.

But the problem facing the young couple in contemplating a date for the wedding was that Philip was uncertain about the direction of his career. One thing the young lovers had in common was that they both came from middle-class families that were feeling the financial pinch. Both had fathers who were no longer in the workforce. They could not look to their families for any assistance. This might have been an argument for staying put in the public service, but in 1926 he quit the Probate Office in an attempt to improve his position, and went to work in a public accountant's office. It is clear this was something of a disappointment, and, when he still had to sit for his final exams for the Commonwealth Institute of Accounts, he changed jobs again, this time for a post as accounts general clerk with the British Imperial Oil Company.

One month later he applied for a commission in the Stores and Accounting Branch of the Royal Australian Air Force. It seemed like an impulsive decision – and he was a man susceptible to impulses – but perhaps the idea had been simmering in the back of his mind. At a time when the romance of air flight had captured the public imagination there was a certain glamour attaching to the recently established RAAF; the lad who had been proud of his appearance in long'uns might even have even appreciated that with his height and looks a uniform would suit him. And the RAAF did, like the public service, offer security of employment. Nevertheless joining the only recently formed Air Force was a break with the past, a career change which would capture the attention of friends and family.

Filling in the application form he listed his parent's nationality as 'Australian', but adding 'both of English descent'. Putting himself down as single, he did not mention forthcoming marriage. Among the accomplishments he listed in his application were French, Latin and higher mathematics studied at school. And there was music: 'I play the piano and have been a church pipe organist for 8 years'. It was a safe bet this was an accomplishment not shared by many RAAF officers.

What might have given him cause to hesitate was that it would almost certainly mean, at least in the short term, separation from Pearl, as the RAAF was headquartered in Victoria. On the other hand, the matter of his career would be resolved and planning for the wedding could begin. He had no trouble passing the RAAF exam, and in January 1927 Philip became

Pilot Officer Rickard. It was as if he had acquired overnight, not only a career, but a new identity; he would feel less in the shadow of his two elder brothers, Jack, now practising as a solicitor, and Bill who, with a friend, had just founded an engineering firm.

Although, with his accountancy qualifications, he was destined for the Stores and Equipment branch, Philip underwent a flying training course, a necessary induction into the mystique of the infant Air Force. While he was on this course at Point Cook the Duke and Duchess of York arrived in Melbourne. The royal couple – the Duke, of course, was a decade later to become George VI following the dramatic abdication of his elder brother, Edward – were visiting Australia to preside over the opening of Canberra in May 1927. There was a nice symmetry to this: the Duke's father, George V, when he was Duke of York, had opened the first federal parliament in 1901, the moment captured in Tom Roberts' famous painting.

The RAAF was much involved in Victoria's welcome to the Duke and Duchess on 21 April, a Thursday, when the *HMS Renown* sailed up the Bay, berthing at Port Melbourne. Indeed, the newest of the armed services was hoping to capitalise on the visit, as the Duke was the first member of the royal family to have a formal association with the Air Force, the Duke having requested a transfer from the Navy during the War.

As the couple were welcomed ashore and began a circuitous royal progress via St Kilda to the city, thirty aeroplanes were involved in elaborate flyovers. There was a festive atmosphere over bay and city, heightened by the remarked-upon happy coincidence that back in England their little daughter, Princess Elizabeth, was celebrating her first birthday.

In spite of grey weather and the threat of showers hundreds of thousands of loyal Melburnians lined the route. As the triumphal progress reached its conclusion, the car bearing the royal couple entered the grounds of Government House where they were greeted by the Governor-General Lord Stonehaven and Lady Stonehaven. The Duke then inspected the usual guard of honour, this time provided by the RAAF. He had just completed this ceremonial task, and was no doubt looking forward to a cup of tea or something stronger, when a terrible thing happened. Seven planes were flying low in close formation over St Kilda Road, performing a movement known as the royal salute. As the Duke turned to say something to the guard commander, there was a crack like a pistol shot from the sky, and looking over the commander's shoulder he saw two of the planes collide and fall to the ground in a trail of smoke. 'Two of your buggers gone,' the Duke was heard to remark.

One plane fell into Dodd Street, the other crashed through the roof of the nearby garage of the postal department. Both planes burst into flames, killing the two pilots and the two other airmen on board (a photographer on one plane and a mechanic on the other). Thankfully there were no other deaths or injuries: no one was in the immediate vicinity in the garage where the plane fell through the roof, and those in Dodd Street were able to scatter as they saw the other plane coming down. A macabre footnote to the drama was provided by other pilots who saw the accident from the air and, according to the *Age*, immediately began performing 'a series of hair-raising stunts'. The *Age* reassured its readers that this reflected 'the unwritten law of the British and Australian air forces. Whenever one of their comrades has been killed they fling all their energy into stunts, in order "to keep their tails up", as an Air Force officer remarked after the tragedy.'

Understandably this unfortunate accident cast a blight over the celebrations; it was also the kind of publicity the new service did not need. It compounded concern about the safety record of the RAAF which had, over the last year or two, suffered an alarming number of accidents and fatalities. The *Argus* saw the 'lamentable event' as 'part of the great toll which modern progress makes upon human life' and speculated whether 'a careful examination of the temperaments of candidates for the flying school' might be needed. 'The line between courage and recklessness is difficult to draw.' Not having at this point completed the training course, Philip was not involved in the flyovers in any capacity, but he was probably on the ground in Melbourne to see the pilots, some of whom he had met, perform their heroic rituals of welcome. He might well have felt some relief that, regardless of whether or not he could fly a plane, his career was going to be in the more mundane world of stores and equipment.

Two days later, while the royal couple were preparing for a Saturday at the races, the four dead men were buried. Here the lines of class were observed. The officers were buried at Brighton Cemetery, and the RAAF training school, Philip no doubt included, was in attendance. The two other men were interred, with less ceremony, at Fawkner Cemetery across the river. The coffins of all four airmen, however, were draped with the Union Jack, still Australia's official flag. (The Australian ensigns, in so far as they were promoted by the Labor Party and the Catholic Church, risked being associated with disloyalty.)

Monday was Anzac Day, and it was no accident that the royal itinerary allowed for the Duke and Duchess to be in Melbourne for the occasion. The ceremonies of Anzac were still evolving, and up to this time the march had not become an annual event. However agreement had just been reached that the Day should be a public holiday, and the royal visit was the trigger for organising a Melbourne march of ex-servicemen both as a demonstration of Australia's emerging sense of nationhood and its recommitment to the imperial cause. The march, held in the afternoon, attracted an estimated 30,000 ex-servicemen. The Shrine of Remembrance was yet to be built, so the march began at Princes Bridge and progressed through the city to Parliament House, where the Duke took the salute, and on to the Exhibition Building for a memorial service.

Because of the large numbers marching, this service, originally scheduled to begin at 3.30pm, was late in starting. The crowd, already filling the immense space of the Exhibition Building, grew restless and some rowdy ex-servicemen began to sing 'old war-time songs'; at one point the band struck up with a number described by the *Argus* as 'more popular than polite'. It was 4.30 before some order was restored and the service began. Anglican Archbishop Lees presided, assisted by representatives of the Methodist and Presbyterian churches and the Salvation Army. A notable absence was Catholic Archbishop Mannix or, indeed, any representative of the Roman Catholic church. Catholic ex-servicemen would have been advised not to attend this neo- Protestant service which, in its lack of explicit Christian references, did allow for the participation of the Jewish Sir John Monash, the distinguished general who had been the corps commander of the AIF. In his speech Monash saw Gallipoli as instantly welding the people of Australia into a nation. The Duke, on the other hand, did not touch on Australian nationhood, and saluted the Anzacs for giving their all for King and Empire: 'that great test of arms and the heroic deeds of all who shared in it will be remembered as long as the Empire lasts'.

Not being an ex-serviceman, Philip would not have marched, but he was likely to have watched the impressive procession, and may well have been at the Exhibition Building service. He would have been thinking of his brother Tom, the family's sacrificial offering to King and Empire. And it may have occurred to him that he, on the brink of marriage, was now close to the age that Tom had been when struck down.

In August Philip, as his Record of Service put it, 'passed for Wings'. With air flight still something of a novelty an ability to fly an aeroplane added to the image of the young air force officer. And the forced separation from his lover might have for Philip taken on the character of a lenten preparation, almost a rite of passage, for their long awaited union which would take place on 1 October.

But for Pearl it was a difficult time. She experienced a bout of depression which was much more than the sadness and anxiety of separation. Indeed, the heavy cloud which descended upon her, reducing her to sudden torrents of tears, seemed inexplicable. Years later it would be diagnosed as cyclical depression: but this was its first grim visitation. Was it in any way a legacy of the rheumatic fever of her childhood? Or was this disturbance of her psyche triggered by nervousness at the step she was taking? There was, after all, the memory of her own mother's unhappy marriage, and her sister Sybil's wedding day tears. But ultimately there was no explanation for the depression. It simply had to be borne and lived through.

Philip knew about Pearl's father: it could hardly be kept a secret from him. Indeed, probably at the time of their engagement, Pearl had taken him to the Gladesville Mental Hospital to meet her father; there was a sense, in spite of William's incapacity, of observing the formality of seeking his permission. He was remembered as being kindly disposed to the couple. It seems he was no longer deemed a threat to others. At some stage Edith was told that it would be possible for her husband to come home. She refused to have him back.

So William was not at the wedding to take his daughter down the aisle. If Will had been alive he would have performed that duty; instead it was Les, less than two years her elder, who genially undertook to give the bride away.

It was not a big social occasion – Ryde was hardly Darling Point – but the wedding of Flying Officer Philip Rickard and Miss Pearl Bragg did merit a newspaper report, under the heading of 'AIRMAN'S WEDDING'. The airman, however, was wearing a dark suit; at this stage he probably did not have a formal dress uniform. The bride was described as wearing 'an old world gown of ivory taffeta and silver lace, mounted on pale pink georgette. The train of pink rucked georgette was lined with silver lamé and diamanté with feather trimming.' The bride's 'lovely Limerick lace veil' was noted as having been lent by her aunt, Mrs F J Johnson (the same kind aunt who had sent parcels to Will in France). The bride carried a shower bouquet of roses, carnations and lily of the valley. She was attended by one bridesmaid and two 'little maids', the daughters of her two sisters. Sybil sang during the signing of the register.

The newspaper might have described Pearl's wedding dress as an old world gown but it had a very modern look – the skirt reached only to the knees. Somehow this dress signalled that the marriage of Philip and Pearl would be very different from those of their parents. The modern aura of their wedding was heightened by the romance of Pearl marrying an 'airman'. As they walked down the aisle to the joyful strains of Mendelssohn's Wedding March there was a sense of throwing off the burden of the past, their families' chequered histories, and stepping out into a new world of hope and promise.

Chapter 2

ENGLAND: 'HOME'

I like to think of your English years:
reading Jane Austen after tea,
country walks in Hampshire lanes,
gooseberry fool at the rectory.

Picnics with sherry and spirit lamps,
all wearing Harris tweed,
eating sandwiches on a rug,
Betjeman-land indeed.

Cathedral-crawling in the car,
just making evensong,
country-house visits and dinner
announced by resounding gong.

In the old photo
you wear a fur coat
and just out of view
there's a child taking note.

— Barbara Fisher

Pearl and Philip began married life in Melbourne, but in mid-1928 Philip was
posted to Richmond in New South Wales where Barbara was born in 1929. Life
in the enclosed RAAF community in Richmond was a little racier than what they
were used to in suburban Ryde. In 1932 the Navy, Army & Air Force Journal

carried a cartoon image of Philip, in uniform, merrily playing a pipe organ. It also noted that 'socially he is always in the thick of things, and has the popular regard of those in the service'. 1933 saw them back in Melbourne; John arrived in 1935. They were fortunate to be bringing up their small family relatively unaffected by the Great Depression. And then came what in 1935 would have seemed the opportunity of a lifetime: Philip learned that he was to be sent to England to attend a year-long course at the RAF Staff College. The young Rickard family would be transplanted in Andover, a market town in Hampshire, where the Staff College was located. The Empire called from across the sea.

Pearl and Philip were excited to learn that they were to travel on the RMS *Orion*, a new ship built specifically for the Australian run. The *Orion* was already well known, because it had been launched in December 1934 by the Duke of Gloucester in Brisbane transmitting a signal, by means of radio, to Barrow-in-Furness in Lancashire, where the ship had been built. Taking advantage of the Duke being on a tour of Australia, the Orient Line was making use of modern technology to publicise the launching of its new ship. At over 23,000 tons it was the Line's largest ship and its interior design was sleek and modern, very much a break from the traditional brand of shipboard opulence. The stylish art deco finish was heightened by much use of chromium and bakelite, materials which had the advantage of being resistant to the effects of sea air. And with the journey through the tropics in mind, the *Orion* was the first ship on the Australian run to boast air conditioning in its dining rooms. According to the *Architectural Review* it was 'a landmark in the evolution of the modern liner'.

In November the Rickards travelled north to Sydney to say their farewells to their families and friends before boarding the *Orion* on its maiden voyage back to England. Sea travel dramatised the journey from dominion to mother country, still known to many Australians as 'Home'. The departure on the month long trip involved a unique Australian ritual. Relatives and friends flocked to the wharf, the chance to see over a new ship like the *Orion* being an added attraction. There were presents and flowers and chatter. As the hour of departure approached the visitors were shepherded back on to the wharf and the gangplanks pulled away. Cascades of streamers were thrown, forming a gaudy web linking ship and shore. Philip and Pearl stood on the deck with six-year old Barbara and John, a babe in arms, waving their goodbyes; at one point Philip, smiling broadly, held John up above his head, and from the shore it looked as if there was a risk of the baby being dropped in the water. Last minute jokey messages were shouted from the wharf and probably not heard in the general clamour. It was a time for tears and laughter. And then the blast of the ship's horn heralded the departure and tugboats began slowly to manouvre the ship away from the wharf, the streamers stretching tenuously across the water and snapping one by one. With this symbolic separating from the land the journey had begun.

Philip and Pearl were travelling first class – he was, after all an officer, if only a flight-lieutenant – so this moment was the beginning of a high adventure. Usually dinner on the first night was relatively informal, but, once at sea, in first class you 'dressed' for dinner. These weeks at sea afforded an atmosphere of glamorous holiday, a leisurely overture to the Old World. But the ports of call, once the Australian mainland had been left behind, served also as an introduction to Empire. Colombo in Ceylon (as Sri Lanka was then called) was tropically exotic and yet reassuringly British; Aden, in 1935 still governed as part of India, seemed more utilitarian as a port of strategic convenience; the Suez Canal, a French project over which the British had gained control, was the imperial lifeline. Naples provided a 'continental' interlude, but Gibraltar returned the traveller to the imperial network. The ships of the P & O and Orient Lines were themselves part of the imperial experience.

Knowing how important their time in England would be for them, Pearl had brought with her a small 1936 diary. It was beautifully appropriate, therefore, that on 1 January she was able to write her first entry:

> Our first glimpse of England. Dropped anchor at Plymouth. Surprised to see cultivated slopes right to water's edge.

The following morning the *Orion* berthed at Tilbury and by 11.30 they were at St Pancras. They had expected to be met, but, finding no one from Australia House at the station, had to go in search of a hotel themselves, first to the Strand Palace which was full, before taking a room at the nearby Waldorf. It was 'very tiring with a baby in arms'. Pearl noted that the Waldorf was 'very comfy' (their room had its own bathroom, a comparative novelty for most Australians) but 'quite pricey'. They went out for some lunch and a stroll down the Strand to Australia House. The traffic, Philip observed, was 'amazing' with 'buses everywhere'. On this walk Philip went into Boots Chemist, an English institution, and bought a large Boots 'Scribbling Diary', its foolscap pages conveniently interleaved with blotting paper. They would both be recording the day-by-day detail of their lives in England.

This was the merest glimpse of London, for after one night of Waldorf luxury they were on their way to Andover. The town, 'with its narrow streets and quaint houses', seemed satisfactorily English. In the afternoon they inspected the house, 'Little Steps', a two-storey Edwardian pile, which had been arranged for them, and after one night at a local hotel they moved in. The wife of an RAAF colleague, Peg Ewart, had called on them in the morning at the hotel, and had, it seemed, given them a quick introduction to the kind of life they could expect to lead in Andover, because she undertook to try and get her maid's sister to 'do' for them. Ethel turned up the next evening: Pearl, who had never engaged a maid before, thought she seemed to be 'the right type'. Within a few days Philip was remarking, with regard to Ethel's weekly afternoon off, that it made them 'realise just how indispensible is domestic help, with children at any rate'. By the end of the week they had booked Barbara into a small nearby private school, 'Westholme', run by a Mrs Gardiner, who impressed Philip by having studied in Paris. So, within nine days of their arrival in England, they had been effortlessly slotted into a particular form of middle-class, home-county life.

There was one difference, however: their immediate circle, from which most of their friends and acquaintances would be drawn, was associated with the Staff College. There would be some similarities to the service life they were used to in Australia, but the College was itself an imperial institution, so that they would be meeting couples from other parts of the Empire, most notably Canada. But, as they would soon discover, in spite of the atmosphere of service life and the input of the dominion visitors, the social conventions of this imperial community were decidedly English.

If Pearl and Philip had read *The Times* on 1 January they would have detected a mood of guarded optimism. In spite of the Italian invasion of Abyssinia (Ethiopia) and the ineffectual response of the League of Nations, *The Times* thought that 1936 could 'be faced without misgiving, provided that recovery at home is not interrupted', the problem being the likelihood of industrial disputes, particularly in the troubled coal mining industry. The Prince of Wales, on the other hand, announced that he was hoping to visit more of the occupational clubs for the unemployed: it was 'a cause that lies very close to my heart'. On 2 January Goebbels, who as Germany's minister for propaganda was one of the Nazis' leading anti-semites, was quoted as saying that 'in a disturbed and turbulent world Germany was like a tranquil and placid island of internal and external peace'. Yet the resignation of Britain's High Commissioner for Refugees in Germany had just been announced; his 'devastating' report into 'the persecution of Jews and others' was suppressed in Germany.

But such international concerns soon gave way to a royal drama. By 18 January it was clear that King George V was ailing. Pearl noted that 'The King's Illness', as the headlines described it, was 'causing some anxiety'. On that day Rudyard Kipling, the great poet of Empire, died. Meanwhile the King, who was passing in and out of consciousness, was reported to have asked, 'How is the Empire?' His secretary reassured him that all was well with His Majesty's Empire; the King smiled and lapsed into unconsciousness. The message conveyed was that the King could now die in peace. Two days later at 9.25pm the famous announcement was posted that 'the King's life is moving peacefully to its close'. Five minutes before midnight, in the presence of the Queen, the Prince of Wales, the Duke of York, the Princess Royal and the Duke and Duchess of Gloucester, the King joined Kipling in death.

That, at least, was the official story. We now know that the King's last words were 'God damn you!' addressed to the nurse who had just given him a sedative. The King's physician, Lord Dawson of Penn, recorded in his diary that he later administered a lethal injection of cocaine and morphine, mainly so that the royal death could be announced in *The Times* in the morning, rather than in the less respectable evening papers.

With the announcement, the BBC immediately suspended its usual broadcasts, an exception being made only for shipping forecasts and gale warnings. Theatres and cinemas closed. In Andover, however, news of the King's death did not prevent Pearl from keeping an appointment with the hairdresser to have her hair 'permanently waved': 'Quite an ordeal. I was in the chair for 4 hours – but it certainly looks better.'

A week later they listened to the funeral on their recently acquired wireless set, and it was as if they could visualise what was happening. There was still a sense of wonder at the immediacy of radio and its ability to take the listener to the scene. (According to *The Times* there were sixteen microphones at Windsor, six outside Westminster Hall and two at Hyde Park.) Philip reported:

> Huge crowds watched the magnificent procession. Especially beautiful was the service from St George's Chapel Windsor. Singing was unaccompanied. Never have I heard better chanting (Psalm 23).

In the afternoon they went for a walk to nearby Hatherden, 'a typical village of thatched cottages', where they saw a charity school for poor children, endowed in 1725, and, he noted, 'still in use'. If they felt, courtesy of radio, that they had witnessed an historical national event in the morning, picturesque Hatherden offered a sense of social history on their doorstep, alive in the present.

There was one more thing needed to equip the family for life in Andover – a motor car. Philip tried a Baby Austin and a Ford 8 and settled on the latter. It was, of course, a great aid for getting around and for sightseeing, but the road toll might have given them pause for thought: in the London area alone over a thousand people were killed and 55,000 injured in 1935. That the great majority of those killed were either pedestrians or cyclists suggests that many had still not adapted to the increasing motor traffic; perhaps, too, it reflected the number of new, inexperienced drivers taking to the road. Philip was not new to driving, but he still had to undergo what he thought was an exacting test. (The question of Pearl learning to drive never arose.)

Pearl and Philip seemed to adapt easily to English social life. 'Calling' was a required social ritual for the wives, and perhaps useful in a community that was changing annually. The unofficial rule was that a call should last for no more than a quarter of an hour; and if the person called upon was not at home a card was left. The call would then need to be returned. It was the 'colonials' who were most likely to break or stretch the rules. Mrs Tackaberry, a Canadian, insisted that Pearl stay to tea when she called: she was 'very nice and easy to talk to' and the usual fifteen minutes became an hour and a half. Once these introductory rites had been performed there were for the women more informal encounters, such as morning coffee at Priscilla's teashop in the High Street and afternoon tea parties.

They were soon making friends. Their immediate neighbours, Eric and Margaret Brand, were English: he was a Commander in the Royal Navy and was either attending or auditing the Staff College course, though for what reason is not clear. They were, according to Philip, 'a charming couple who seemed intent on helping us to adapt ourselves to English conditions'. They lived in some style, as was evident from a dinner party they hosted:

> Everything done in the proper! way. Maid announced us ... Sherry before. Maids waited on table – anything you wanted to drink, nice dinner, & the ladies left the gents to have the port & coffee. Later the Commander showed some films, some he had taken of his ship "Courageous" & their naval happenings, & others of the Jubilee Celebrations. A great way of entertaining one's friends.

It was such an occasion that provoked the comment: 'We think either or both of them must have means.' Indeed, Pearl and Philip, who were themselves mindful of the cost of things (Philip often recorded prices in his diary), could not help assessing the financial means of the people they met. Encountering another hospitable couple who had a butler, maid and nanny, not to mention an Alvis car, Philip concluded, understandably, that they 'must have money'; it was refreshing, however, that 'they seem unaffected'.

The Rickards did not attempt to compete with formal dinner parties. For them, and for most of the friends they made, the standard form of evening hospitality was the sherry party, with up to twenty invited for sherry (occasionally cocktails) and savouries. Afterwards some might, after a quick bite, go on to one of the local picture theatres. Andover was not a big enough town to have its own repertory theatre company, so the 'pictures' (the American term 'movies' was never used) were particularly popular. Pearl and Philip, like most of their acquaintances, were avid picture-goers, and in their diaries the films seen would be noted, usually with a pithy appraisal. There were also cosy evenings by the fire, listening to the wireless or reading. Jane Austen was perhaps Pearl's preferred comfort reading – an appropriate choice, as Hampshire was Austen territory.

As winter edged into spring golf and tennis made their appearance. One of the social advantages of the course at the Staff College was that it allowed a fair amount of free time for study or recreation. Both Philip and Pearl had played social tennis in Australia, and Philip a little golf, but Pearl had never ventured onto a golf course. In Andover she clearly felt a need to take it up. Golf shoes having been bought, she played a round or two with Philip, confessing that 'our form was awful, particularly mine'. She was encouraged to take some lessons. 'I intend to try very hard,' she dutifully promised herself after her first lesson with the pro. She even practiced golf shots in the backyard (as she called it) of 'Little Steps'. But alas, one lesson had to be abandoned because her hands were sore and blistered; it left her feeling 'rather fagged' and her enthusiasm for golf, never, one suspects, very serious, wilted.

Tennis they could both enjoy, and their neighbours, the Brands, had a grass court, but Pearl found herself drafted into a women's tournament at the College which was something of a trial. For someone who usually looked for the best in people, Pearl was moved to make one of her more pointed comments. It was, for May, a cold day, and Pearl observed, with perhaps some satisfaction, that Mrs Shapcott, one of the better players, 'looked chilly in her shorts'. There was an implied judgment, too, about appropriate attire for a woman on the tennis court.

On weekends they were often busy sightseeing, and given their shared interest in church music cathedrals were high on the agenda. Salisbury and Winchester were both within easy reach and they visited them regularly. On Easter Sunday they went to Matins at St Mary's, Andover's parish church, but the real excitement of the day was Evensong at Salisbury. On his first visit Philip had thought the cathedral interior 'rather cold and bare', but for Easter it was ablaze with spring flowers. With a procession it was 'a fine service', Philip approving the singing of the choir and the organ playing. When visiting a cathedral or church he would always hope to seek out the organist – and organists are a kind of fellowship – and it was a cause for joy to be invited up to the console to see as well as hear the organ being played.

But their most ambitious touring was a seventeen-day motoring holiday in August, undertaken with another Australian couple, Alan and Jean Walters. The children were left in the care of Ethel, assisted by a temporary nursemaid. Philip was the driver (it was his car) and he kept a travel diary of their tour which took them through Wales, the English Lake District, Glasgow, the Scottish lochs, Edinburgh and home through the eastern counties. 'We propose to do the tour as cheaply as possible', Pearl wrote, and with a carrier attached to the Ford 8 for their luggage, the car was also filled with picnic gear for their alfresco lunches. They were constantly on the move, never spending more than a night in one place. (Indeed, they appeared to survive for the seventeen days without any recourse to a laundry.) In the course of the trip they managed to add nine cathedrals to their tally, not to mention the odd parish church, abbey or ruin; one wonders whether the Walters fully shared the Rickards' appetite for England's religious heritage.

At the end of the trip Philip typed up the diary, fifteen foolscap pages, which was designed not only as their own record, but to be circulated to their families in Australia. It concludes with a classic expression of the Australian appreciation of England:

> So ends a wonderful experience – 2,300 miles of England, Wales and Scotland – sights and experiences we shall never forget – things we have both dreamed of since we were children, but scarcely ever believed we should have the luck to see with our own eyes.

Just one year earlier the young Robert Menzies, on his first trip to England, had voiced a remarkably similar, if more grandiloquently phrased, sentiment in his diary:

> At last we are in England. Our journey to Mecca has ended, and our minds abandoned to those reflections which can so strangely (unless

you remember our traditions and upbringing) move the soul of those
who go 'home' to a land they have never seen ...

It was 'traditions and upbringing' that had prepared Pearl and Philip for the
first-hand experience of England.

Seeing England was their first priority: continental travel would have
to wait. But they could not help but be aware of what was happening in
Europe. The Brands had visited Germany and showed them the film of
their tour. They went again in August, possibly taking in Hitler's showpiece
Olympic Games in Berlin. A good Australian friend they had made on the
Orion, Kath Gordon, also made a trip to Germany and told them all about it.
There was clearly much interest in what was happening in Hitler's Germany.
There were those who found much to admire. Menzies, for example, while
conceding that totalitarianism was 'not suited to the British genius', praised
the 'really spiritual quality in the willingness of young Germans to devote
themselves to the service and well-being of the State'. When Pearl and
Philip did later make travel plans they were not tempted to go and see for
themselves – Paris was much more alluring.

In his course at the Staff College Philip was being constantly reminded of
the possibility of another European war. At a nearby establishment devoted
to researching chemical warfare his class experienced 'a good mock-up of a
gas bomb attack' and were put through 'a light concentration of various gases
including mustard'. They visited aircraft factories and at Farnborough 'saw
quite a lot of new and hush hush things'. There were interesting lectures on
the air forces of Germany and the Soviet Union, and in one exercise he was
called upon to mount a critique of the 'German Air Plan'.

There was, however, no sense of imminent crisis. The RAF air pageant
at Hendon could be enjoyed as an entertainment and social occasion
('wonderful strawberries'). The experience of England was to be savoured
and stored up for later recollection.

Although there was no doubt about the importance of England for them,
Pearl and Philip were also noting the things about England and the English
which irritated or repelled them. Philip found many of the English officers
on the course a frustrating lot. It was not long before he had decided that
the head of his syndicate was 'an old woman', and his limited capacity for
patience was tested by team exercises. 'These English blokes talk a hell of a

lot and get nothing done,' he complained. What was worse, they were lazy: 'one or two doing a fair amount of work and the rest nothing'. It is notable, too, that while Philip found much to admire in English church music his complaint about the choirs he had heard was that they lacked vitality.

They also tired of the in-bred atmosphere of their RAF circle. Enjoying a 'musical evening' with some friends, in the course of which he accompanied Pearl in some songs, Philip remarked that it was a 'very pleasant change to meet some people who like music and can talk about something else besides maids, service talk and so on'. They were alienated by any English suggestion of 'putting on airs'. Pearl thought that the wife of the Commandant was 'a bit artificial', and Philip was scathing about the hostess of a cocktail party who was 'so frightfully bored she spends most of her time in London. Dreadful hardship to have pots of coin, two cars, chauffeur etc.' It was alright to be rich, as it seemed their neighbours the Brands were, so long as you didn't flaunt it.

And in their appreciation of England they were often making Australian comparisons. They were struck by the 'charming situation' of Tintern Abbey, 'close by the river and sheltered on all sides by gently sloping grassy and wooded hills, coloured in vivid greens such as we rarely if ever see in Australia'. But in a postcard to his mother Philip likened parts of the Wye Valley to 'the upper reaches of the dear old Hawkesbury'. In Scotland there was an occasional sense of familiarity, as when they came across 'a bit of scenery with a stream flowing under a bridge – more like a bit of Australia than anything we have yet seen over here'. The seaside, however, was another matter: 'these shingle beaches aren't much chop', Philip complained, and the 'exhausting' Sunday spent driving there made it hardly seem worth the effort.

In Edinburgh they were impressed by the Scottish National War Memorial:

> This is built in the form of a chapel on the highest point of the castle rock … The exterior of the Memorial is nothing remarkable, nor does it stand out like the Shrine at Melbourne or the Sydney Memorial in Hyde Park. The interior is however a splendid piece of work.

It was an interesting time to be comparing war memorials. Melbourne's Shrine of Remembrance had only been completed in 1934, dedicated by the Duke of Gloucester on Armistice Day (11 November). In its dominating position facing down the length of Swanston Street to the Carlton and United brewery, the Shrine, a monolith in a low level skyline, 'stood out' then even more than it does today.

They were, of course, in constant touch with Australia. Receiving mail was always noted and was particularly welcome in the early months: 'so pleased to have some news of home,' Pearl wrote on 27 January. Air mail had just been introduced but was a costlier novelty and not generally used. When Philip received an air mail letter from his sister it was bearing the bad news that their mother was ill. He wondered whether he should reply by air mail, as if it could only be justified in an emergency. (He did.)

As the beginning of their year at Andover had been marked by the death of King George, so the end of the Staff College course saw another royal drama being played out. In June Philip had attended a levee at Buckingham Palace; his outfit was rather makeshift with borrowed field boots and a stick in place of a sword. He bowed to the new King Edward in the throne room as the band of the Irish Guards played 'Danny Boy'. With all the uniforms, gentlemen in court dress and the King in kilts (the levee was an all male affair) it was 'an unforgettably magnificent spectacle'.

A week or two before this levee the names of Mr and Mrs Ernest Simpson had appeared for the first time in the Court Circular. They had attended a dinner, given by the King, where they had met Prime Minister Stanley Baldwin and Mrs Baldwin, both of whom knew that the American divorcee was the King's mistress and greeted her with glacial politeness. The affair was, for those in society, already common knowledge; but, influenced by Lord Beaverbrook, the English press had followed its traditional practice of not reporting such royal liaisons. It was a different matter in the United States and Europe where the affair was the stuff of tabloid gossip. In July Wallis Simpson began divorce proceedings. By November there was a gathering sense of crisis in political circles as the King's intention of marrying Mrs Simpson became clear. Baldwin consulted dominion prime ministers who supported the British Prime Minister in not countenancing a morganatic marriage, in which Wallis would not have been Queen.

On 1 December the Bishop of Bradford, addressing his diocesan conference, spoke of the King's need of divine grace, a comment which was interpreted as a reference to his affair with Mrs Simpson and was reported in some of the provincial press, leading to a breakdown in the press embargo. On 3 December *The Times* broke its silence, and in lofty but vague tones, making no mention of Mrs Simpson, saw the risk of damage to the Monarchy. It pointed to the role of the dominions and described the Monarchy as 'a rock to the world outside amid the seething tide of Communism and Dictatorship'. The following day its report was more concrete: the King had expressed a desire to contract a marriage as would require a special Act of Parliament, which his ministers said was impossible. Therefore, *The Times* made clear, in a superb piece of establishment sophistry, it was not a question of the King's Ministers objecting to his choice of wife. On 6 December, still without naming Mrs Simpson, *The Times* finally identified 'the woman' as a twice-divorced Commoner and American. The next day it condescended to name Mrs Simpson in a small par on page 14, reporting her arrival in Cannes.

Clearly in Andover they had heard of Mrs Simpson, but appeared to be unaware of the gathering political crisis until 3 December, when Philip reports as 'the sensation' the King's wish to marry her. 'Papers are full of it. How is it going to pan out'? At the sherry party they hosted the next day they were all talking about it; it was a cause for 'great excitement'. On 10 December, while Pearl was having afternoon tea with friends, the news of King Edward's abdication came through. Philip chose to see this outcome as a victory for British constitutionalism – 'in other countries it would be 100 to 1 on a revolution'. And in what was for her an unusually declamatory diary entry Pearl wrote that 'the people have been marvellous in this crisis'. She added that everyone seemed to have confidence in the new King and Queen, though her need to mention this suggests that their suitability was a matter for discussion. On 11 December they enjoyed 'a bright little dinner party' at the Brands' before going on to a dance at the Mess, arriving at 9.30. At ten o'clock everything stopped as they gathered round the wireless to listen to Edward's farewell message which Pearl thought was 'moving'. Then the party resumed. 'Danced till 1AM', Philip wrote in his diary. 'Good time'.

Indeed their year in Andover could be summed up as 'a good time', offering a comfortable and privileged introduction to England, its society, institutions and countryside. They had the enjoyment of their two small children but, thanks to the maid, were not over-burdened with the responsibility of looking after them. Andover may have been a parochial community, self-absorbed in its own social life, but it was less than two hours from London on the train. They also knew that they would be having at least one more year in England based in London – in fact, it was to become two years – with Philip attached to Australia House as assistant air liaison officer. There was still much to look forward to.

However, there was one shadow over their happiness. The weariness that had blighted Pearl's golf lessons was a cause for concern. Two weeks after the lesson that had to abandoned, she went to Dr Hodgson who sounded her heart and told her 'not to overdo it at any time', one of those vague injunctions that risks being meaningless. At a later consultation he was more specific. According to Philip the doctor was 'concerned about her heart'. Pearl recorded:

> He has given me strict instructions to take things easy and rest 1½ hours every afternoon – not to keep many late hours and to avoid being fatigued. I don't know how I am going to manage it with children to look after.

It was not a cheering message for a woman who had just turned thirty-three. Although for a time she tried to have the daily afternoon rest it was a difficult regimen to maintain. In the coming years Dr Hodgson's 'strict instructions' might appear to have been ignored, but there was often a nagging regret that she didn't have more energy.

In London, after a couple of weeks in a rather dismal hotel which had the one advantage of having a nursery, the Rickards moved into a 'very warm and cosy' little flat in Leinster Square, not far from Notting Hill Gate. (Barbara had been left to board at Westholme in Andover.) Within a few days they had engaged a maid, Betty, described by Philip as 'a very tall wench and above the average type of nurse maid so far as we can judge'. In their haste to get domestic help they had risked not first getting references.

They had made brief visits to London while at Andover, usually just for the day, but now they had London on their doorstep and there was an exciting sense of being in the thick of things. On their first visit to the Temple Church for Sunday Evensong – a church which, with its famous organist Thalben Ball, would acquire a special place in Philip's musical pantheon – they were moved by the singing and organ playing. But Philip also observed: 'Most peculiar fellow sat behind us. Clad in purple robe & sandals. Long hair but no beard. One should not be surprised at any thing in London.'

Little more than a week after moving in, they came home from evening 'drinks' at the home of another RAAF couple to find the flat in darkness 'and poor little John all alone in his cot'. There was a note from Betty informing them that her mother had been run over and badly injured, requiring her to go home immediately. Pearl's suspicion about this explanation was heightened when she found her gold watch and a £1 note missing. She 'did not sleep a wink' that night. Concluding that Betty was 'a bad egg' they reported the theft to the police. Some weeks later Pearl glimpsed Betty at a crowded

Lyons corner house, but felt powerless to act. This eerie little incident, and its setting, contains a whiff of early Hitchcock, conjuring up the elusive sense of threat that London was capable of evoking.

Pearl was hesitant about choosing a maid this time, and finally settled on an Austrian girl, Maria Ruppitsch, engaging her in the first instance on trial for a fortnight. 'Perhaps we will have more luck with a foreigner,' she noted, though Philip wondered whether the Austrian's English would be up to it. Maria had soon won their trust (and two-year old John's too); with a cheerful smile and a sensible look to her, she soon became an important and dependable member of the household. Later, she would sometimes be included in family outings. She was photographed with the children and won a place in family albums. Pearl and Philip did have better luck with a foreigner: Maria was to be remembered as part of their English experience.

London was to prove an intense cultural experience. There were the great galleries to absorb. At the Tate they appreciated the Turners but did not take to the Epstein sculptures. Nevertheless they were curious enough to visit an exhibition of his work at the Leicester Galleries, where they were taken aback by his 'Consummatum Est' ('It is Finished'). This massively modernist alabaster sculpture presents not a conventional Christ on the Cross but a figure laid out for burial, a heavy Assyrian or Egyptian-looking bearded Christ, the hands open in deathly welcome. In an unusually outspoken response Pearl described it as 'his latest monstrosity', but had to concede that some of his busts of famous people were good. Her Sydney Anglican upbringing had not prepared her for the National Gallery's wealth of medieval and renaissance religious painting which left her rather bemused – 'too many of the Virgin & Child pictures – I do not understand these'. Philip bought *The World's Greatest Paintings: One Hundred Selected Masterpieces of Famous Art Galleries*, a large, authoritative looking tome which took an important place on the family bookshelves.

Music, of course, figured prominently in their agenda. They soon homed in on Sadlers Wells, where opera was sung in English, at first queueing up for standing room. From 'Aida' and 'The Magic Flute' they graduated to Wagner's 'Die Meistersingers' ('splendid performance'), though they found 'Valkyrie' more testing ('so many long pauses with nothing happening'). They made just one visit to the more expensive Covent Garden to see 'Tales of Hoffman', a performance which happened to be attended by the new Queen. Their seats in the amphitheatre afforded them 'a splendid view of her Majesty' who, in the distinctive way she was to make her own, 'looked very gracious and charming'. Attending a performance at Sadlers Wells with their friend Kath Gordon, Pearl had her first taste of classical ballet ('very graceful and the music delightful').

There were marvellous concerts, most notably in the monumentally huge Royal Albert Hall. Their first experience of the redoubtable Sir Thomas Beecham conducting was 'a red letter day'. Philip was impressed that Beecham conducted without a score, 'scourging the players as with whips, and getting the last ounce of perfection'. Pearl was thrilled by the voice of Richard Tauber, but they were both deeply disappointed with Chaliapin who was evidently past his prime, giving a performance which was 'more like a vaudeville act'. (In fact he died a year later.) They heard and enjoyed the notable Australian soprano Florence Austral, whose all too brief career was nearing its end, in a performance of 'The Messiah'. And of course, there was always church music, often with a couple of services on a Sunday, Philip sometimes going on his own. But much as they enjoyed Bach they found the 'St Matthew Passion' a little daunting: 'fine work,' Philip noted, 'but difficult to understand'. (Towards the end of 1937, when they knew they would be having a third year in England, they bought on hire purchase a piano, a Metzler, for 39 guineas.)

Much theatre too. They got great pleasure from Shaw's 'Candida' and 'Pygmalion': Philip thought 'Candida' was a splendid play, but added, 'GBS is a cynical old man all the same'. Particular interest attached to this revival as Candida was played by the American film star Ann Harding. He acquired *The Complete Plays of Bernard Shaw* for the family library. The actors they saw in productions include many of the stage luminaries of that era: Diana Wynyard, Robert Morley, Rex Harrison, Marie Ney, Edmund Gwenn, Edith Evans, John Gielgud, Peggy Ashcroft.

Nor did they ignore popular culture (a term that would not have been used then). Madame Tussaud's Wax Works seemed to be compulsory: 'very interesting' Pearl thought, but the Chamber of Horrors (which was off limits for Barbara) was 'pretty grim', while Philip remarked that he 'couldn't see this stuff being shown in any Australian city'. (Whether he saw this as a good or bad thing is not clear.) Never known to be great followers of sport, they saw Don Bradman score a century at Lords, which was satisfying even if the result was, as so often, a draw. And, as we shall see, Philip also had a taste for more raffish forms of entertainment.

But for Pearl and Philip the great spectacle of 1937 was the Coronation in May. Philip had checked out the Australian Coronation contingent when it arrived in March. He thought the Navy looked 'a very second rate lot' and that the Air Force were 'smartly turned out but not a good looking type'. London was becoming more and more crowded as the date of the Coronation approached, and a strategically timed bus strike made things worse. But the Coronation itself lived up to expectations. They set off at the crack of dawn, armed with their sandwiches for lunch; the train was jam-packed, but they were in their seats in a stand opposite Buckingham Palace, by seven o'clock. They could hardly have asked for a better vantage point for witnessing this imperial extravaganza. They heard the service in the Abbey over the loudspeakers. But the real excitement was the procession returning from the Abbey which reached them at 3.30pm and took an hour to pass. Pearl's diary account strains for superlatives:

> The pageantry of today was an unforgettable sight. The uniforms of the various regiments together with the mounted bands, Dominion Contingents, Indian officers and men in their colourful dress and bright turbans. The Royal Family all looked their best. The little princesses looked very sweet. The Gold Coach in which the King and Queen rode is a most marvellous affair. The greatest thrill of all was to see the King and Queen wearing their crowns on the return journey from the Abbey. The Royal family came out on the balcony of the palace after the procession was over and acknowledged the cheers of the crowd.

Presumably the Australian contingent did not let the side down as Philip might have feared. When it was all over they walked up to Piccadilly, had some early supper, and then, at Philip's suggestion, went to the Windmill Theatre. Pearl conceded that in spite of the risqué jokes and the nude *tableaux vivants* the show was 'fairly entertaining'. After the imperial splendour of the Coronation the tawdry 'nuddy' (as Philip called it) of the Windmill might have seemed almost subversive. But the Empire was not forgotten: the theatre broadcast the King's speech at eight o'clock. And the Windmill was already on its way to becoming a London institution.

In spite of their disdain for English beaches they decided that Bournemouth passed muster. They had sussed it out in April and, although it was 'a big place', thought it 'very pretty' and, importantly, its beach was sandy; 'everything looked fresh and clean'. In August they gave up their London flat, and Pearl and the children, with Maria, came down to Bournemouth and settled in a boarding house. Philip was still at work in Australia House and in bachelor quarters; it was three weeks before he joined the family. This was the authentic English seaside experience: deckchairs on the beach, sandcastles and fish and chips, candle-lit illuminations in the Gardens, the

D'oyly Carte production of Gilbert and Sullivan's 'Yeomen of the Guard' at the Pavilion. And, of course, it was respectable Bournemouth not vulgar Blackpool. There was even the bonus of good weather.

In September they took Maria and the children to Andover: Barbara was returning to school at 'Westholme', where Maria and John would also stay while Pearl and Philip made their first and only trip to the Continent (as the European mainland was always called). With a three hour channel crossing to Dieppe it took a full day to travel from London to Paris; they were glad to get to their hotel, the Hotel d'Ecosse in the Rue d'Edinbourg (a hotel no doubt catering for British travellers), in time for dinner. After their first 'continental breakfast' (coffee and rolls) they headed for Notre Dame cathedral; they spent the afternoon 'tramping round the Louvre', 'a huge place packed with artistic treasures'. Over the next week they took in many of the sights, from the Pantheon and St Chapelle to the Eiffel Tower. They had a day in Versailles ('a monument to the extravagance of the French kings'), an afternoon in Chartres ('really magnificent stained glass') and 'Rigoletto' at the Opera House ('a gorgeous theatre'). Their visits to the Paris Exhibition were relatively brief, and they only glimpsed the monumental German and Soviet Union pavilions which dominated it, facing each other in symbolic confrontation. They did not see the Spanish pavilion where Picasso's 'Guernica' was on display.

Philip was determined that they would sample Paris nightlife. They saw the legendary Josephine Baker at the Folies Bergère and were not particularly impressed, but, Philip remarked, there were 'lots of lovely nudes – spectacular show, but pretty garish & b.a. [bloody awful] music'. On another night they did a select organised tour of nightlife which, from 9.30pm to 2.30am, took them from an underground student dive to a Moslem club, an apaché dance hall, a cabaret, winding up at another nude show. Perhaps this was too much of a good thing, as Philip concluded his diary report with a rather dutiful moral coda: 'All right for one night, but this Parisian gaiety is an artificial and unhealthy existence'.

Much as they appreciated the urban grandeur and impressive monuments of Paris, they did not seem to warm to the French. At Chartres Pearl could not help noticing that 'the Cathedral itself looks very dirty inside', adding that 'so many of the French churches need a good cleaning out'. In Paris they felt it was more difficult to get 'good cheap food' than in London. When they crossed the border into the lake and mountain scenery of Switzerland Philip immediately discerned 'the change from French slovenliness to Swiss neatness and tidiness'. Their hotel was 'awfully clean', its food 'tip top', and, best of all, they 'enjoyed lovely hot baths after going dirty in Paris'. And yet Paris *was* Paris. The following year, as a special treat, Philip took nine-year-old Barbara to Paris for a long weekend, which they both hugely enjoyed.

At the end of their two week trip Pearl wrote in her diary: "Phil and I have both enjoyed our trip immensely, but it is good to be back in England once more'. England, if not their home, was nevertheless Home.

The holiday season was over, and for their remaining time in England they found a flat in Orsett Terrace, which was close to the Kensington neighbourhood they were familiar with. It comprised the second and third floors of a terrace house, the rest of the house being occupied by the landlord, his wife and their small child. The Colwills became good friends, and their similar family situation provided a bond. Barbara was placed in a nearby Catholic convent, where she would later be a boarder for a term. In spite of the still pervasive sectarianism in Australia it was not unknown for Anglicans and Protestants to hold a convent education in some esteem.

One of the institutions that was useful to colonial visitors to England was the Victoria League. Through the League the Rickards were able to sample the kind of England that they had only glimpsed in plays or films. They were the guests of a Captain and Mrs Stocker for a long weekend at 'Northlands' on their estate (pedigree cattle) near Chichester. They were met at the railway station by the chauffeur. Captain Stocker was 'very deaf but good old stick', Mrs Stocker charming. They dressed for dinner which came with 'lots of lovely silver' and 'plenty of maids', but, Philip observed in the Stockers' favour, 'no side'. There was a little local sightseeing and some tennis; Pearl enjoyed lazing in the lovely garden, but Philip soon found the quietness a bit oppressive. After dinner there seemed no alternative but to go to bed: 'couldn't stick these evenings for long', he confessed.

A rather different experience, courtesy of the League, was a sherry party at the home of the celebrated writer of romantic fiction, Elinor Glyn, notorious for her identifying sex appeal as 'It'. She was also a patriot, as Pearl reported:

> Mrs Glyn gave a short talk which amused us a good deal. She kept saying 'Thank God I'm English' in the course of her talk. She is an extraordinary looking woman – 72 years of age – a well preserved mask like face & masses of lovely red hair, which looks natural enough. The people present were mostly from the Dominions & included 12 young

air cadets from Australia & several students from India & other parts
of the Empire.

One wonders what the Australian air cadets, let alone the Indian students,
made of Mrs Glyn. Pearl and Philip had been in England long enough to
characterise the purveyor of 'It' as a colourful English eccentric.

You never knew whom you might meet or see in London. One day Pearl
was taking John in his pram (it was probably Maria's afternoon off) on his
daily visit to the Round Pond in Kensington Gardens when a distinguished
looking woman with a small entourage in her wake paused to take a look at
the pram's contents. 'What a beautiful child!' she exclaimed before moving
on. A woman observing the incident made a point of informing Pearl that
the child's admirer was none other than the British-born former Queen Ena
of Spain, grand-daughter of Queen Victoria, exiled from Spain since the
advent of the Republicans in 1931.

Like most Australians in England, Pearl and Philip would compare notes
with Australian friends about the English. They could cope with, indeed
even share, the English devotion to dogs, but the doings of these pets on
busy London streets was another matter. Indeed cleanliness generally was
a concern for these hygiene-conscious Australians, though the English
were clearly not as culpable as the French. From a colonial perspective the
English, who did not necessarily realise that their Empire was already in
decline, could appear self-satisfied: 'how the English love themselves'
Philip remarked more than once. As for the Church of England, in spite
of their attachment to it and their appreciation of its glories, Philip saw it
as complacent and lethargic and needing a bomb placed under it. And it
often took some time for visiting Australians to appreciate that London and
the Home Counties were only one version of 'England'. Their brief passing
glimpse of the slums of Glasgow shook them: 'Never have we seen such
obvious signs of unemployment, such hordes of unwashed and ill fed kids in
the streets, such dire poverty'. This was not the 'green and pleasant land' they
had been brought up to expect.

Philip had been in the RAAF for ten years. He passed a promotion exam
in 1937 which raised him to Squadron Leader and which he saw as no
more than his due. But his irritation with the hierarchical bureaucracy of
the Force mounted with the years, particularly as he saw the Stores and

Equipment Branch as tending to be ignored or taken for granted by the top brass. Nor was he much impressed by the Australian Defence Minister, Sir Archdale Parkhill, whom he met at tea at Australia House – 'typical pot bellied politician with not much grey matter in my opinion'. It seemed as if his frustrations with the Service made home life more important than ever, particularly as they were so far away from Australia. With two children it is clear that there was no intention of adding to their number; Pearl's health may have been a consideration, but it also made sense for them to opt for the modern nuclear family, a decided contrast to their own family backgrounds. For Pearl, in her often difficult and stressful childhood it was possible for a child to be lost in the crowd. With just two children – and this was the kind of family size enjoyed by most of their friends – they had more time and affection to give them. They were both loving and devoted parents, Philip taking particular pleasure from giving the children treats or presents, whether Barbara's weekend in Paris or the Hornby train set, a Christmas gift for both children, though one suspects for himself as well.

Usually sociable and good humoured in company, Philip was capable of what might have passed for flirting with women in their set. But is it possible that he flirted a little with Maria too? Or, indeed, with the 'tall wench' Betty during her brief stay? (His use of the word 'wench' has an odd, ambiguous ring to it.) If so, these were situations with an entirely different social dynamic. In August 1937 he was baching for three weeks in London while Pearl, Maria and the children were at Bournemouth. The fact that his diary for this time has many blank pages might tempt one to be suspicious – as if he was necessarily 'up to something' – when the most likely explanation is that he was having a rather dull, lonely time. Certainly Pearl showed no sign of concern: indeed, she notes receiving a letter from 'Filipo', the name recalling the lover who wrote her songs and poems.

Their social life in London was not as regular and organised as it had been in Andover, and Pearl, being at home, was the one more likely to be experiencing loneliness. The friendship with Kath Gordon was important for them both, but particularly for Pearl. Kath had a circle of women friends, a lively bunch of teachers and nurses mostly living in 'digs', and Pearl enjoyed their company, but it was Kath's warmth and generosity of spirit that attracted her. When Kath's departure for Australia was imminent in August 1937 Pearl writes, with an almost audible sigh, 'How I shall miss her!'

There was, however, still much to do and see. Always careful about her own appearance, and interested in fashion, she enjoyed shopping. She made some of her own dresses, which helped the family budget, but there were occasional more extravagant purchases. In midsummer, with Philip in tow, she looked at fur coats, finally settling on a 'natural musquash' costing 20 guineas; presumably Philip's approval was needed for this investment. 'Hope it will be a success'. The shop agreed to store it for her until she needed it in the winter. 1930s fashions suited her, she wore her clothes well, and, with a hair style similar to Wallis Simpson's (and she was often thought to resemble the Duchess of Windsor), she would have looked perfectly at home in the streets of Mayfair. With her acquired poise she was clearly attractive in a way that was not so obvious before. One day when she was exploring Westminster Abbey on her own 'a young chap', apparently sightseeing like her, struck up a conversation; next thing he was suggesting lunch and a show. 'I didn't want to hurt his feelings, so told him as nicely as I could that I had a lunch engagement with my husband.'

For Pearl – and indeed for Philip too – what came to be seen as the climax of their three years in England was her Presentation at Court. Friends had brushed distant shoulders with Royalty at Buckingham Palace garden parties, which were huge gatherings where genteel stampedes were possible, and the relative intimacy of an evening Presentation definitely ranked much higher in the Royal stakes. These occasions were less formal than they had been in earlier reigns, and, unlike the presentation of debutantes, did not involve any choreographed ceremony. But considerable preparation and investment were required, as is evident from Philip's account:

> The great day – Pearl's Presentation at Buckingham Palace. 8.20 saw us leaving by car (Armstrong Siddeley) complete with Chauffeuse & Footwoman – Pearl in v. lovely gown of dawn pink satin & self in court dress. After a little waiting in the Mall [we] were got into the Palace & waited with lots of others in the gold drawing room. HMs came in a little after 10PM while the Regimental Band continued soft music & walked among the guests – a delightfully informal affair. E. looked v. beautiful and G. v. brown & well. Then supper & bubbly in a room with fabulous gold plate on view. After leaving Palace, visits to 2 photographers & home tired out about 3AM.

The room in which the Presentation took place was in fact the White Drawing Room, a dazzling John Nash creation in white and gold. A cunningly disguised mirror-covered door, leading into the private apartments, allowed the Royal Party to make a low-key entrance. Philip's hired court dress included the compulsory sword, white gloves, gaiters and buckled shoes. But of course it was Pearl's dress that was all important – a slim, stylish gown of the period with an elaborate, tucked bodice, and worn with full length gloves, drop earrings and a modest tiara. (In Edwardian times feathers and a train had still been called for.) Pearl could hardly afford to relax over the supper with the all-important photographs still to come. In these Philip looks just a little pleased with himself, but there is also a suggestion of a mildly ironic 'How about this outfit!' Pearl, on the other hand, is the complete fashion plate: just the merest hint of a smile, elegantly relaxed, her almost languorous gaze directed slightly away from the camera. Such photographs were routinely relayed back to Australia, and, indeed, Philip and Pearl appeared in their Presentation ensembles in the pages of the Sydney *Sun* a fortnight later, much to the satisfaction of their families.

In London Pearl and Philip were becoming increasingly aware of the ideological drama being played out on the European stage. One Sunday evening while they were singing hymns at Evensong at St Martin-in-the-Fields, which faces Trafalgar Square, there were huge crowds outside being addressed by the British Fascist leader Sir Oswald Mosley. They knew where they preferred to be. On another Sunday they passed a big procession of Communists, Philip feeling the need to record that it was 'very orderly'. While Germany indulged in the choreographed theatrics of its Nuremberg rallies and the like, Britain was not beyond responding in its own way. In 1937 Kath got them tickets for a massive Festival of Youth held at Wembley Stadium. Before a crowd of 60,000, thousands of children representing youth organisations from throughout Britain marched, sang and performed callisthenics. The event was presided over by the Royal Family. The commentary to the British Pathé newsreel made clear the agenda. 'How different this is from some of the mass meetings we've seen in other parts of the world,' the voice proclaimed. For here it was 'the legions of peace' which were 'on the march'.

All this came home to the Australian couple in a personal sense when in March 1938 Nazi troops marched uninvited into Austria, which was promptly integrated into Germany. Soon after this annexation Maria was one of many Austrians in England rounded up for a day on a German ship where they were given a crash course in their newly acquired nationality. Maria was clearly receptive to the new order. She came back to Orsett Terrace her eyes aglow with patriotic fervour, proclaiming the greatness of

'Die Fuhrer'. In July she left the Rickard household to go home. She was not heard from again.

In September there was a gathering sense of crisis as Hitler fixed his gaze on democratic Czechoslovakia, demanding the secession of its Sudetenland which bordered Germany. The policy of Appeasement, supported by British prime minister Chamberlain, *The Times* and much of the establishment, was being put to the test. Trenches were being dug in Hyde Park and people were being prepared for the wearing of gas masks. The brief euphoria following the signing on 30 September of the Munich Agreement, which effectively handed Czechoslovakia to the Germans, was short-lived. It was not long before the justification of the Agreement shifted to the necessity of buying precious time to re-arm for the inevitable war.

All this must have alarmed Philip and Pearl as they wondered whether they might be stranded in England. Could they have been in the crowd which saw Chamberlain on his return from Munich sharing the balcony of Buckingham Palace with the Royal Family? There is no way of knowing as Pearl's diary for 1938, if she kept one, does not survive, and Philip virtually gives up keeping his in July, almost as if they felt that they had, for all intents and purposes, 'done' England, and were now impatient to be on their way back to Australia.

He briefly resumed a diary in January 1939, the month of their departure. They saw the New Year in sitting up in bed and 'drank to the future in some Australian port'. Barbara and John were sniffling with colds: 'both the kids need some Australian sunshine'. On their last Sunday Philip took Barbara to the Temple Church for 'a last look'. The choir, singing part of Bach's Christmas Oratorio was, as usual, 'in splendid form'. On 20 January they were packing up to the very last minute; indeed Philip had to rush out to buy two more suitcases. There was quite a crowd to see them off at St Pancras Station – 'lots of sweets, books etc. and flowers'. Their ship, the P&O *Strathallan*, sailed from Tilbury at eight o'clock. While 'the children were very thrilled and full of questions', for their parents this voyage could not have quite the excitement of the *Orion* in 1935. But they were returning with a rich store of 'sights and experiences' – 'things we have both dreamed of since we were children'. They were bringing their own England back with them, and their three year stay in the Home Country would leave its imprint on their marriage. It was a happy, even blessed, time before things started to go wrong.

Chapter 3

MELBOURNE:
THE WOMAN IN THE RED COAT

How wretched you made us, old charmer,
and how good to have you around
when we felt you belonged to us

and not to the woman in the red coat
Mother and I saw you with
that day in Little Collins Street.

We'd withdrawn into the entrance
of a chichi little shop – avoiding,
I suppose, embarrassment,

though nothing was said. Always
I've remembered this silent retreat
and the red coat receding

on my father's arm.

— Barbara Fisher

On the travellers' return to Australia Philip was posted to Melbourne, where they
rented a Spanish Mission bungalow in High Street, Glen Iris, a suburb which
saw much development in the inter-war years. One of the drawbacks of service life
was the frequency of moves. At the end of the year the Rickards found themselves
in Richmond near Sydney where they had spent five years early in their marriage.
Their stay this time was brief. In April 1940 they were back in Melbourne, moving

into what was described as a maisonette in East Malvern. One year later Philip was sent to London as assistant air liaison officer.

Sometime between their arrival back in Australia and Philip's departure in 1941 Pearl decided that she would discard the name that had been imposed on her at baptism and adopt her second name 'Mildred'. She had never liked 'Pearl', possibly thinking it a bit vulgar or 'common'. (Significantly, Ray Lawler was later to call one of his barmaids in *Summer of the Seventeenth Doll* Pearl.) So for Philip, and for new acquaintances, she was now Mildred; but for family and old friends she could not escape being Pearl. Nevertheless becoming Mildred was mildly liberating, offering a new, perhaps more independent way of thinking of herself.

Mildred and Philip were at home on 3 September 1939 when prime minister Robert Menzies, speaking on the ABC, solemnly announced that Great Britain had declared war on Germany and that, 'as a result', Australia was also at war. As far as Menzies was concerned, Britain still spoke for the Empire. Mildred's mother, Edith, happened to be staying with them at the time – she was, in her later years, gradually losing such independence as she had had, and would soon be, as the family sometimes wryly described it, 'humping her bluey' around her daughters' and sons' homes. Also staying with the Rickards was a young niece, Pauline, who was about Barbara's age. They were both at the frenetically giggly stage, but remember how the seriousness of the occasion silenced them. But it was their elders who appreciated what it might mean for Mildred and Philip – and, indeed, for other members of the wider family.

Yet there was a sense of unreality about the early months of the conflict, particularly in Australia, so distant from the European arena; and in 1939 there was none of the jingoistic enthusiasm which had marked 1914. The 'phoney war', as the first months came to be known, ended with the sudden fall of France in mid-1940, but there was still concern in government circles in Australia about poor morale in the community, sometimes seen as a legacy of the Great Depression.

Back in Melbourne after the brief stay in Richmond, the family settled into the modern maisonette in Nott Street, East Malvern, not so very far from Glen Iris. At a rental of £5.10.0 a fortnight, it was a comfortable, two-storey semi-detached dwelling in a quiet street; a walk across Central Park took you to the tram stop on Wattletree Road. Barry Humphries was later to mark Glen Iris as Sandy Stone territory, but in the 1930s it was a suburb which attracted young married couples. East Malvern had a rather statelier ambience, and the pair of maisonettes might have seemed, for those comfortably ensconced in their federation houses, an unwelcome intrusion. (And even the use of the term 'maisonette' has a slightly Edna Everage ring to it.) But for the Rickards it was an appealing locality for a young family. As well as Central Park, nearby were the picturesque Hedgeley Dene Gardens, the very name suggestive of their deliberately English prettiness. It was the kind of park where you would not have been surprised to run into Christopher Robin.

In 1941 Philip was posted back to London as assistant air liaison officer at Australian House; no doubt his familiarity with the British RAF scene would have been an advantage in wartime. But, in the war context, there was no question of the family accompanying him. He was also being sent via the United States and Canada with a schedule which included visits to aircraft factories: the United States, of course, was not at this stage itself at war.

He was to travel by sea to Vancouver, and Mildred accompanied him to Sydney from where the ship, the Canadian Australasian Line *Aorangi*, was sailing on 22 April. The Australian rituals of farewell were abandoned in wartime: there was nothing to celebrate about this voyage. There were no streamers; indeed, relatives and friends were not allowed on the wharf, let alone on board the ship. Nor was it any comfort to know that the Line's other ship on the Pacific run, the *Niagara*, had sunk off the New Zealand coast in June 1940 after hitting a mine. It might seem understandable, then, that there was an element of tension in the departure. But Philip's first letter home, posted in Auckland, hints at a different source of uneasiness:

> Dearest Sweetheart,
> I am only just beginning to realise that I am actually on my way to the
> other side. The goodbye yesterday seemed so unusual in a way. There
> were so many things I wanted to say to you that didn't get said. I am
> not often at a loss for words but yesterday morning I just felt dumb.
> You looked very lovely my dearest, and you were very brave too. I can
> write now what I couldn't find words to say then, that I truly love you
> more than words can say.

There may have been other family members present, but was that sufficient to explain why he was 'at a loss for words'? What prevented him from saying that he loved her 'more than words can say'? What was it that made him feel dumb?

His pen did not linger with these thoughts; there was still a sense of things unsaid as he moved on to describe the ship and the beginning of their journey. The liner had an escort which followed them down the harbour, then, once at sea, took up position some distance ahead, zig-zagging from time to time to confuse the enemy. There was also a group of RAAF trainees on board, bound for Canada under the Empire Air Training Scheme. And with his first letter Philip instituted his system of numbering each letter on the back of the envelope with the date of posting, so that in the course of their correspondence it would become clear if any letter had gone missing.

But it was easy to put these reminders of war aside and relax into the familiar laziness of sea travel. The ship was 'a lovely vessel' – faster and more comfortable, Philip thought, than the *Orion* and *Strathallan* – and he had 'a de luxe single deck cabin with a beautiful private bath room'. The ventilation was so good that the blackout caused no inconvenience. The food was 'absolutely first class and so far as I can see menus and service are peace time standard', and there was cinema at night. The trainees were 'a good bunch of young fellows', but not much was seen of them as they were fed separately, and parts of the ship, such as the lounge, music room and library, were out of bounds to them.

The ship berthed in Auckland on Anzac Day, in time for the march, which the RAAF trainees took part in. Philip was well looked after during their four day stay in port, both by the CO of a nearby Air Force station and by a farmer whom he met in a hotel lounge ('the people here are very friendly and hospitable') who took Philip, along with his daughter, to lunch and the cinema ('The Thief of Baghdad'). Philip fitted in Sunday morning Matins at the Anglican Cathedral where the Governor, who happened to be Marshall of the RAF Sir Cyril Newall, read both lessons. And there was time for a quick overnight trip to Rotorua to glimpse the maori village set amidst the geysers of boiling mud and the springs emitting their clouds of sulphurous smoke. The countryside he passed through, with its green rolling hills, reminded him of 'parts of the south of England', except for the interruption here and there of the distinctive form of an extinct volcano.

The next morning he was taken for a drive around Auckland by 'a girl from the Women's National Service Corps', a 'Miss Rosemary Carr' as he formally describes her. The view from One Tree Hill of the harbour with its ferries prompted the inevitable comparison with Sydney: 'some day it will probably have a bridge to add to the resemblance'. After the drive he was lunched by the Carrs in their 'comfortable 2 storied weatherboard house set in pleasant grounds with a good view of the harbour'. With his usual appraising eye he concluded from the beautifully furnished house and the presence of a maid that the Carrs were 'pretty well off'; but, he assures

Mildred, 'they have absolutely no "side" and are very hospitable'. The people he spoke to in Auckland – all relatively well-to-do like the Carrs – were 'very scathing in their opinions of the NZ socialist government, most of whom I believe were pacifists & sedition merchants in the last war – some of them spending a good time in the jug'. It is perhaps no surprise that Philip and Mildred, and, indeed, most of the Rickard and Bragg families, were in the habit of voting for the anti-Labor parties.

Back at sea tedium began to set in. He was sharing a table with a medical officer, a nurse and a flight lieutenant – 'about the three driest people I have ever had to dine with'. The medical officer actually went three days without saying a word. As they approached the equator the heat became oppressive, particularly with the blackout conditions at night. It now emerges in Philip's letters that the *Aorangi* was effectively a troop ship. At least on this leg of the voyage there were only two women on board – Joyce Brown, who was accompanying her RAF officer husband, and the nurse, Sister Smith, who was attached to the RAAF draft. One night there was a concert, which, as Philip explained, being an all male affair, meant that some of the items were 'a bit on the risky side'. Joyce Brown insisted on attending; 'the poor nursing sister had to go too to save her face'. In spite of this embarrassment the concert was deemed a success, put on by and for 'the men'; officers did not contribute.

As they approached Vancouver, Sister Smith, who was returning on the ship to Australia, agreed to take back some small birthday presents which she would post to Mildred – six pairs of Canadian stockings for her, and a pendant bought at Rotorua, made of specially treated Kauri gum with a little sea shell, coral and maiden hair set inside it, for Barbara.

The ship stopped at Victoria, enough time for a brief tour of British Columbia's capital city, before berthing at Vancouver. The RAAF contingent were met by Air Vice Marshal Goble, whom Philip had met in England. Goble, a distinguished air ace from the Great War who in 1924, with another officer, had made the first successful flight around Australia, had been appointed chief of the air staff in 1939, but had, within months, resigned the position in acrimonious political circumstances, making do instead with the position of Australian air liaison officer to the Empire Air Training Scheme in Canada. Philip respected Goble who was 'friendly and approachable' and that evening had 'a long yarn' with him 'in private', where they seem to have compared notes on colleagues they disliked. Philip made a point of telling Mildred that Goble had inquired after her and the children.

Philip had little time for sightseeing, though he sent six-year-old John 'a folder of Vancouver views'. The trainees were travelling by train across the

Rockies, but Philip was surprised to learn that Goble had arranged for his travel in Canada and the United States to be by air. He went down to the railway station to see Goble and the Browns off and reported that 'Joyce was complete with brand new Canadian fur coat which must have made a hole in Brown's pocket'. He also took in the scene at the station with its low platforms, the Pullman carriages, the massive engines with their clanging bells and 'the ubiquitous negro porters with their familiar jovial round faces and rolling eyes': even though this was Canada and not the United States it was a bit like finding yourself in an American movie.

'The next day I was off by air into what it is difficult to realise sometimes is a foreign country.' He was travelling as a civilian and would be living out of a suitcase for several weeks; his trunk, with his uniforms and gear, had been sent on to Ottawa. His first destination was San Diego. A 14-seater Boeing took him to Seattle where, having passed through Customs, he boarded 'a huge 21 seater Douglas' which flew to San Diego, landing on the way at Portland, Sacramento, Oakland, San Francisco and Los Angeles. The all-day flight did not get him to San Diego till 9pm, and, with all its stops, might have seemed exhausting, but for Philip this kind of commercial flight was a novelty. He was impressed that 'morning coffee, hot lunch and hot dinner [were] all served in mid-air'. And at San Diego he checked into a hilltop hotel which on its top floor had a 'sky room' with an elaborate cocktail bar and lounge commanding a view of the city and harbour. Hotels in Sydney and Melbourne did not run to 'sky rooms'.

The next day was spent at the Consolidated Aircraft factory which, with a workforce of 16,000, was making flying boats – some for the RAAF – and four-engine bombers for the RAF. Then it was on to Los Angeles, which was his real introduction to America. Philip was surprised to learn that the airport, then at Burbank, was fifteen miles from the city centre, but only five miles from Hollywood: how could he resist booking into a hotel in 'the Movie City'. He spent several days at the Lockheed factory; indeed his hosts lent him a 1941 Chevrolet to help him get around the widely dispersed outposts of Los Angeles. The British Aircraft Commission, which he needed to visit, had its offices in Beverley Hills; and the huge Douglas factory, which was also on his agenda, was twelve miles away at Santa Monica. The scale of America was daunting:

> When I got to the Douglas factory I found a huge place crowded for miles around with cars parked on both sides of the street & on every vacant bit of land. They have about 25000 employees & I reckon about ⅔rds must

own cars. You have no idea of the volume of private car traffic in USA. Of course the main roads are wide – at least 3 lanes of traffic each way, while the Federal Highways are amazing. The road to the airport lies along a Federal Highway for some miles & this part consists of two separated one-way roads – side by side – & five cars can drive abreast each way!

A Lockheed representative took him out for a night on the town. They dined at the popular 'Beachcomber' where the food was Chinese, but the lights were so dim that he couldn't see what he was eating. Sound effects, such as the illusion of rain falling intermittently on the roof, contributed to the tropical ambience. Afterwards they went to a 'Folies' variety show 'consisting of low comedians & leg shows'. Philip's ambivalence towards such entertainments surfaced again: 'I didn't like to tell the fellow who took me but I think the audience should have been paid instead of charged'. On the way back to his hotel they dropped in on another café where a negro vocal quartet were 'really worth listening to'. It was their 'infectious sense of rhythm' and, as with the porters at the Vancouver station, 'the way they roll their eyes' that attracted him.

He had never seen so many bars and cafes as in Hollywood, and he carefully described the logistics of the drive-in cafés, unknown in Australia. When he heard the whine of police car sirens it was 'exactly as we get them on the screen'. Some of the police – 'real tough guys' – were on motor cycles; they all carried automatic pistols in holsters. If this impressed rather than disturbed him, it seemed to be because it confirmed the image of America created by the movies.

And, of course, there was Hollywood itself. He drove around the streets of Beverley Hills in his borrowed Chev admiring the homes of the stars. He was struck by the absence of fences; the mansions of Mary Pickford and Charlie Chaplin were exceptions, boasting walls and gates 'to keep out the curious'. He visited the Will Rogers Ranch which, for 25 cents in aid of the Salvation Army, you could inspect. It was 'a very lovely old place of homely design'; he noted that the much loved Rogers, who had died in an aeroplane crash in 1935, had been mayor of Beverley Hills.

Philip also spent a day at the Fox studio, where a film about the RAF was being made. (Almost certainly, this was 'A Yank in the RAF', directed by Henry King and starring Tyrone Power and Betty Grable. It was about an American pilot who joins the RAF to impress a former girlfriend, but who gradually comes to appreciate what the Allies are fighting for.) It was his visit to the Fox studio lot that provoked an appraisal of American women:

The movie colony probably has a Bohemian influence on clothing fashions & habits generally. Slacks of all kinds are very popular with young and old girls. Most of the women folk strike me as being very hard in the face – not nearly as attractive as the Canadian women I saw in Vancouver. Make up is pretty thick. But for really tough looking ladies you should see some of the movie actresses. Add their speech plus gum chewing to their make up & you get something a good way removed from my idea of feminine charm … Betty Grable, although she has a stunning figure, looked as tough as barbed wire.

Los Angeles was not without more elevated culture. He was impressed by the Hollywood Bowl, which he had seen in a technicolour film featuring the conductor Stokowski, and regretted that its program of symphony concerts, opera and ballet did not commence until July. And at the cinema he was fortunate to see the original two-hour Fantasound version of Walt Disney's 'Fantasia', which was only shown in a handful of specially equipped cinemas in the United States. Philip reported with interest that the three main speakers at the screen were supplemented by 64 speakers around the theatre. Although he didn't comment on Disney's animation, he thought the music, which ranged from Bach's famous Toccata and Fugue in D Minor to Stravinsky's 'Rite of Spring', played by the Philadelphia Orchestra conducted by Stokowski, was marvellous. RKO was to take over the film's wider release, so that what Australians were later to see was a much shorter version without the technical brilliance of Fantasound.

Philip clearly relished this heady experience of the wonders and oddities of Los Angeles, and it provoked one of his longest letters to 'Dearest Sweetheart Mildred'. It was a month since he had left Australia and he had no expectations of mail before the east coast. He enjoyed sharing his travel stories with Mildred, but in the midst of his pleasure there were hints of anxiety. 'Believe me, as time & distance separate us more & more I realise more & more just how much you mean to me my darling – my true & only love'. And in his next letter he dared to ask: 'How much do you love me darling because I love you so much & you are such a long way away.'

Philip was now due to fly east to New York. He discovered that it was easy enough to organise an overnight stop in Salt Lake City, Utah. The attraction was the city's Mormon Tabernacle which was well known around the world through the regular broadcasts of its Sunday morning services, featuring its large choir and four-manual organ, and although he knew little about the Mormons, who were very few in number in Australia at that time, as a keen organist Philip could not let the opportunity to visit the Tabernacle pass.

His hotel was on Temple Square, his room affording an excellent view of both the Temple and the Tabernacle. He had not appreciated that these were two distinct buildings, the Temple being 'the Mormon Holy of Holies like Solomon's Temple was to the Jews', only accessible to the elect, while the Tabernacle was the site for public worship, from where came the world famous broadcasts. He also needed to explain that the Mormons' official name was the 'Church of Jesus Christ of Latter-Day Saints'.

The Tabernacle was a large, squat, unprepossessing structure, but its oval-shaped interior, seating 8000, was remarkable for its all-timber roof, constructed without metal bolts or screws; nor did it require internal pillars to support it. The effect, Philip thought, was one of 'spaciousness and intimacy combined because of the marvelous acoustics'. The Sunday morning service was 'a truly thrilling experience'. As well as leading the hymns, the choir of over 300 sang three choruses from Mendelssohn's 'Elijah', including 'Lift Thine Eyes'; the organist boomed forth with Cesar Franck. He thought it extraordinary that there was no collection or offertory until it was explained to him that the church operated on the tithe system. Salt Lake City might have seemed another American oddity, yet its Tabernacle's powerful musical program was reassuringly conventional. Philip's reporting of the Tabernacle's music led to him to ask Mildred if she had started singing lessons again. 'I do so miss your singing and no piano to sit down to.'

After this Mormon interlude Philip took an overnight flight to New York. The Douglas airliner was fitted out with sleepers:

> ...upper & lower bunks on both sides & you sleep with head to the nose of the plane and toes to the tail. It's for all the world like the pictures you see of Pullman sleepers on American trains in films.

In New York he was booked into the Commodore Hotel which, at $4 a day, was 'on the expensive side', but was conveniently located, close to Grand Central Terminal. His room was on the nineteenth floor, but as he pointed out, this was nothing in the city of skyscrapers. In travelogue mode he felt the need to explain the geography of New York; in 1941 he could not assume that Mildred would know that 'the city and some of the residential districts are actually on an island called Manhattan'. He penned a rough map of the island, marking Central Park, Fifth Avenue and Broadway, which breaks up the symmetry of the street grid.

His first port of call was the British Purchasing Commission Office, catching up on the progress of the large orders placed by the Australian

Air Board. But that evening he was taken out, along with two colleagues from the British office and their wives, to a night baseball game. Their host was a US Army Colonel, Christie. They passed through Harlem to get there – 'niggers everywhere'. The huge ground was 'brilliantly floodlit like day'. He was amazed to learn that some of the players earned more than $10,000 a year. He was particularly struck by the way the 40,000 crowd all stood up at one point of the game 'to unstick their behinds for a few minutes', a national custom, 'the seventh-innings scratch', it was explained to him.

On a brief working trip to Washington – flying there and back in a day – he had time only to register that it was 'a place of magnificent public buildings'. A Commander Fahrney invited him home to dinner; they lived in Chevy Chase which, with its leafy woods and green lawns, was 'beautiful – you might be in the south of England'. He was delighted to learn that the Fahrneys were musical: 'he sings tenor and she accompanies – they have a Steinway Grand'. A shared interest in music always helped establish rapport. At dinner they were waited on by a negro butler, who was not, however, given to rolling his eyes.

Back in New York he was taking in museums, art galleries and, of course, churches. The unfinished Episcopalian cathedral of St John the Divine he thought 'more impressive than beautiful'. He looked in at St Patrick's cathedral, 'a rather fine Gothic church spoilt by cheap looking glass & all the other things the RCs have'. He was impressed by St Thomas's Episcopalian church where he attended Choral Communion. The music was 'grand' and the preacher didn't sound a bit American: 'one might have been at church in England or Australia'. He dropped in on Evensong at the Church of the Transfiguration, popularly known as 'The Little Church Around the Corner', which he had heard about as being the church which 'theatrical folk' attended. He had got the impression that it was Roman Catholic and was pleasantly surprised to find that it was actually Anglo-Catholic Episcopalian. He could appreciate the Englishness of its tiny churchyard in the middle of high-rise New York.

He made the compulsory trip to the top of the Empire State Building, and walked down Broadway at night. The blaze of lights was dazzling, but up close the street was 'tawdry and dirty'. Most of the theatres were actually on streets off Broadway, which instead was lined with 'cheap dancing joints, amusement parlors, cocktail bars and grubby cafés'. The street was 'swarming with Jews and toughs'. He was struck by the men, often smoking cigars, in their 'loud two toned shoes' and wearing straw boaters or panamas with colourful bands. Most women seemed to roll their stockings, even below the knee; boys wore knickerbockers, and children were often dressed in a style which Australians would have found old-fashioned.

As in Los Angeles he clearly enjoyed recounting his experience of America, its colourful extravagance and vitality; the sense of familiarity created by the movies at times undermined by the shock of cultural difference. But beyond the casual racism directed at Jews and blacks, common for the time, he showed little awareness of the ethnic diversity of America. It was the immensity and the energy of the place which commanded his attention.

For over six weeks his letters home had been a kind of intermittent monologue: 'you can imagine just how I am looking forward to my first letter from home', he wrote, concluding his letter of 1 June.

The very next day he received his first two letters from Mildred. 'On opening them and reading them it was like taking a long deep bitter drink.' He was being reminded of his fall from grace – the 'affair' back in Melbourne, which he had so carefully skated around in his letters home, and which had cast a shadow over his departure. Whatever protestations of regret and remorse he had made, Mildred could not easily forget it. In her loneliness in Melbourne she was haunted by the sense of betrayal.

The woman in the red coat has no name. What little we know of her, and the affair, comes from Philip's anguished reply to Mildred's two letters.

It must have started some months before his departure in April. For Barbara to have been present, the incident in Little Collins Street must have taken place in January during the school holidays. The woman in the red coat mixed in RAAF circles, as she was known to one of Philip's senior colleagues, Hugh Wrigley. Perhaps she worked as a stenographer for the RAAF. Or could she have been the wife of a pilot who was serving overseas? Philip depicts her as a siren figure:

> This affair just simply snared me in a sort of web of fascination before
> I had the sense to see it. She was attractive and had a certain gaiety
> of manner and she just wouldn't leave me alone – rang me daily at the
> office and wrote me notes. I told her repeatedly that it was wrong and
> foolish, that I really loved you and that anyway there were the children
> whom I loved too. Twice I wrote her saying we mustn't see each other

again and that she must stop ringing and writing me. Shortly after each time she waylaid me and started all over again.

The affair seemed to have come to an end, however, but then, when 'waylaid' by her yet again, he mentioned that he was shortly to go overseas and found himself surrendering once more to 'the web of fascination':

> The resultant flattery made me forget my resolutions. After that Saturday morning, I wrote her saying what a mess my foolishness had landed me in, and above all how it hurt you at a time when you most needed strength and courage to face the future. I didn't see her, or write to her again, although she did try to get in touch with me through Hugh before I left Melbourne. That was the end of it, although I did receive another letter at Auckland .... She wanted to know why we couldn't write to each other and what harm that would do to anyone. I tore the letter up and didn't reply to it, but in a letter to Hugh Wrigley from Suva, I told him about it and asked him to explain to her if he should see her that it was the end of this foolishness and that enough mischief had been caused already. But please don't embarrass Hugh by speaking to him about the affair. I am truly sorry that all this has happened.

It was unworthy of Philip to shift the blame for the affair on to the woman in the red coat, and at one level he appreciated that in doing so he was depicting himself as weak and malleable. He admitted that Mildred's 'pages and pages' of reproaches were 'justified':

> I know I deserve them all & have no right to expect you to love me the least bit. But believe me, I do love you so much and do long for just a word of love in your letters. When you sign 'your dutiful wife', it sounds like a stranger speaking – small comfort for a man leaving his family for an uncertain time. I know my love for you just can't be reconciled with the way I have hurt you. It was your misfortune to have married a man who just isn't worthy of your love – I've got too many bad traits.

It was humiliating for Mildred that at least one of Philip's colleagues should know about the affair. Mildred was also concerned that Philip had forgotten to pay a fortnight's rent in April before his departure, and suspected that he had not wanted her to see the cheque book for his account; he had used all the cheques in this book, but had taken the butts with him.

It was as if she thought that he might have made a cheque either in favour of the woman in the red coat, or perhaps in respect of a gift for her. (Mildred herself was using a joint account.) In his reply Philip carefully copied out the details of all the cheque butts for March and April, and protested that he had simply overlooked a fortnight's rent. As well he might have, if, in the midst of preparations for his departure, he was still leading this double emotional life. 'There you are and you can believe or not. I can't blame you if you don't.'

After this tortured litany of self-abasement and explanations, Philip goes on to comment on Mildred's Melbourne news, particularly relating to the children, and to add a little about his own activities, but the tone is flat and perfunctory. He was finishing the letter at 1am in the morning. 'I'll close this rotten letter before I tear it up.' He still concludes with 'love & kisses' but cannot resist taking his cue from Mildred's letter and signing as 'Your dutiful husband Philip'.

Philip was thirty-eight at the time of the affair. He and Mildred had been married for thirteen years. His unnamed lover may have been 'attractive', but he knew that he, too, with his good looks and sociable manner, was attractive to the opposite sex. That gave him a certain confidence in social relationships with women: it is unlikely that he was simply manipulated into the affair by the artful machinations of a temptress. If he saw himself as having sexual needs – and he was a man with a very active libido – which were not fully accommodated in his marriage, this was something that would be painfully difficult to communicate, particularly in a letter; and in any case, for a man of somewhat conventional morality the self-centredness of such an explanation would have been repugnant. Was it easier to confess his 'bad traits' in general terms and convict himself of being unworthy of Mildred's love?

The last few days in New York were 'infernally busy'. Philip was writing a sixteen-page report of all his work in New York which he posted off to the Air Board before moving on to Ottawa, where Air Vice Marshal Goble was stationed. Writing from Ottawa on 11 June Philip apologised for his last letter. 'It <u>was</u> a miserable letter and probably had a depressing effect on you but that was a reflection of how I felt at the time.' But without any further comment or reflection he moved immediately onto his Ottawa news, as if he had satisfactorily dealt with the legacy of the affair and could put the pain and embarrassment of it behind him.

And he did have news of interest to Mildred. The Brands, their neighbourly friends in Andover, were living in Ottawa, and Philip spent a weekend with them. Eric was now 'a full blown captain – four rings of braid' – and Margaret was 'blooming as usual and expecting'. Her first pregnancy had ended in tragedy when the baby choked suddenly four hours after birth; subsequently there had been a miscarriage. 'Aren't they hard triers', Philip commented. He assured Mildred that 'notwithstanding the Canadian surroundings, the Brand ménage is still definitely and distinctly English of the naval flavour'.

For most of the time he was staying with Goble's assistant, Squadron Leader Lawson, a bachelor, who threw a small cocktail party for him. Philip thought Lawson's apartment was 'rather pretentious for a young bachelor by Australian standards, but then American and Canadian standards of living are lavish and expensive to our ideas'. On his last night the Gobles, who were also known to Mildred, had him to dinner. They drank champagne and partook of 'an enormous turkey'. He asked Mrs Goble if she would be kind enough to drop Mildred a note and she readily agreed.

Philip enjoyed his week in Ottawa, partly because it provided the opportunity to catch up with old friends, whereas in the United States he had been mixing with strangers. He appreciated, too, reacquaintance with 'some English/Australian habits which are not observed in USA – for instance morning tea before rising, bread and butter knives, marmalade in a jar on the table and a lot of other small things we are accustomed to'. The familiarity of these 'small things' was comforting: British Canada was less foreign than the United States.

He had been in North America for a month, and for an Australian abroad had had privileged access to aspects of American life and culture in that interesting, hesitant time before Pearl Harbour catapulted the United States into the war. His experience of America would be remembered and recalled, the postcards revisited, though of course the unhappy background to this trip was not mentioned, at least not in front of the children.

He now faced a possibly hazardous sea journey to England. He spent a night or two in Montreal, giving him the briefest glimpse of the other

Canada. 'Tomorrow I set off from here for the other side by ways and means that cannot be disclosed.' He bought tea, sugar and tinned butter to take with him; he was also carrying parcels for the Brands and Gobles. He was amused that toilet rolls were in demand in England. Goble joked that they were going to write their letters to English friends on toilet paper, 'being careful to write on one side only'.

Because of censorship he could not, in his letter, name the port of departure. But he knew that on the ship he would be in charge of troops bound for the war. The journey took him to Scotland via Iceland, which had been occupied by British forces in 1940 in the fear that Germany might have been considering invading it. At this time Iceland had something resembling dominion status under the Danish crown. Like Denmark, Iceland was neutral when the war began, but when Denmark was overrun by the Germans in 1940 Iceland became effectively independent, still clinging to the vestiges of neutrality.

To begin with, the journey was tedious in the extreme, as the convoy moved through heavy fog, the ship's foghorn blaring out a morse code call every few minutes, to be answered by nearby members of the convoy. Sleep was almost impossible. In America he had had the distraction of work – and indeed of pleasure – to take his mind off things. But feeling like a prisoner in his cabin he 'could do nothing but think and think and go over all the things I wanted to forget and hoped you would too.' The two accusing letters he had opened in New York were still the only ones he had received since leaving Sydney two months ago:

> Please do spare me a little warmth of love and affection if you can, and tell me whether you really do care – not just for the sake of Ba & John – but for our own sakes. Believe me, I am not just gaily forgetting that affair as an amusing incident; I am trying hard to blot out something that was base and weak-minded and cruel to you, the more I have had to think about it. But if I haven't said much about it in my letters it is because I am trying to help you forget too by writing as cheerful letters as I can. You do want me to write, often, don't you?

Soon after penning these plaintive lines there was some excitement. A German submarine had sunk a nearby ship and they were on alert for some hours. Only in the morning did they learn that the submarine had been detected 'hanging around after more victims'. One of the escort dropped depth charges around the submarine, bringing it to the surface, whereupon the escort promptly sank it. The next day there was more drama when one of the escort was caught unawares and 'blown to eternity'. It was almost a relief to have some news of wartime danger to send back home.

In the midst of all this Philip was registering the dramatic news that Hitler had invaded Russia. 'And yet I suppose there are still pacifists, isolationists and others who would have us believe that the Germans are nice people and Hitler loves everybody.' But in bringing the Soviet into the war the news was encouraging, and he believed it would hasten Hitler's downfall.

Philip was writing this letter at sea in the hope that the ship would take a sealed bag back with it to Canada from Iceland, which presumably it did. He stepped foot on Scottish soil on 2 July, the last part of the journey having been accomplished 'by devious ways' which he could not reveal, but in much rougher conditions than on the ship to Iceland: he arrived 'having been bathless for over a week and having slept (or tried to) in my clothes'. He arranged for a signal to be sent to the Air Board reporting his arrival and asking that Mildred be informed. He travelled overnight to London, checked in at the Strand Palace Hotel, and, after a bath and breakfast, presented himself to Australia House, which looked 'practically the same as before – just a bit duller – sandbags and protected windows etc'. It was a very different arrival from the pleasurable excitement of 1936 when Philip and Pearl – as she was then – had taken their first stroll down the Strand. In five years the world had changed – and so had they.

It is possible that I was present that day in Little Collins Street. I would have been almost six, and if it occurred during school holidays I would very likely have also been in tow. But if so, I have no memory of the incident. Perhaps I was too engrossed in the shop window to notice the silent masque being enacted.

Barbara, who appreciated that something significant had occurred, nevertheless has no memory of raised voices at home or any suggestion of tears and drama. Whatever were the repercussions that night, or later, our parents were careful to shield us from them.

Indeed, I have happy memories of Nott Street. There is a photograph of me merrily riding my tricycle down the footpath: my father has captioned it, 'Nott St 1941'. It was one of the family photographs he took before going away.

For me Nott Street is identified with 'The Children's Session' on the ABC. This program, instituted in 1939, was already popular with middle-class families and was compulsory listening in the Rickard household. Barbara and I would be sprawled on the lounge room floor, watching the glowing dial panel of the wireless, impatiently waiting for the Session's lively theme music:

Come, Old Mother Hubbard and Jack and Jill
And Tom the Piper's son
Leave your cupboard forget your spill
We're going to have some fun ...

And an hour later the carefully crafted fun and games would come to a musical close:

A jolly good night to every one
A jolly good night to all especially you: and you and you and you ...
and you.

Somehow my childhood memories of 'The Children's Session' are encased in the warmth and security of the home – the suburban peace of Nott Street, the neatly contained comfort of the maisonette, toys on the lounge room floor, the smell of cooking wafting in from the kitchen. For when the orchestra played the program's 'going out' music it meant that dinner couldn't be too far off. The four of us, the family unit, would sit down at the dining room table together. There was a sense of benign order to family life.

And yet beneath this well ordered surface there was an undertow of unhappiness which I have no memory of recognising.

Philip's failing to name the woman in the red coat was deliberate, and his description of her – 'she was attractive and had a certain gaiety of manner' – indicates that she was not known to Mildred. But RAAF social life constituted a tight little circle and news of the affair would easily have spread. If Hugh Wrigley knew of the affair, did others? Could Hugh be relied upon to be discreet? And what of the woman herself?

It was Philip's revisiting the affair 'that Saturday morning' that was particularly upsetting for Mildred. The exchange of letters between wife and husband makes it clear that for her at least the matter of this last dalliance had not been satisfactorily resolved before his departure. At their moment of parting he had thought she was being 'very brave'. But perhaps she, like him, was 'at a loss for words', though for quite a different reason. How could she express her disappointment in him? Was this shabby, Saturday morning philanderer the ardent lover who had wooed her with poems and songs?

Communication with each other after Philip's departure was difficult. In 1941 making an international phone call was almost unthinkable. The most one could hope for in immediate contact was the briefest cable conveying greeting or news of safe arrival. The slowness of mail, even with letters sent air mail, was such that there could be little sense of dialogue; even less so, when one of the correspondents was on the move.

On her own in Melbourne, with a household to manage and two children to care for, Mildred had few people at hand she could confide in. Her mother was in Sydney, her sister Sybil in Adelaide, and Kath Gordon, who had become such a good friend in the England years, in Perth. She may have written letters, or made the kind of brief, operator-assisted telephone calls that were the norm then, but these were no substitute for physical contact.

She did have one relative in Melbourne, her Aunty Mill, her mother's youngest sister, after whom she had been given her second name. Mill was married to an army officer, David Blake (known in the family as Dave) who rose to the rank of Major General in the Second World War. They had no children. Mill was a handsome woman, kind hearted but with a brisk manner, and Philip and Mildred saw quite a bit of them during their stay in Melbourne. This was a time of getting to know her aunt, who had not figured prominently in her life. It is possible that she confided in her, but a sense of shame and embarrassment about Philip's affair may have held her back.

It didn't help that John was proving difficult about going to school. Placed in the primary school in Taronga Road, he had taken an instant dislike for his teacher, and had made no friends in the noisy schoolyard. In the morning, when told it was time to get up, his pathetic 'I have a pain' became a familiar refrain. On one occasion at least Mildred physically dragged him, howling, the length of Taronga Road. Aunty Mill had some stern words to say to him.

Mildred had no idea how long Philip would be away. For Mildred, facing this kind of extended separation, the affair in Melbourne did not augur well for the future. What further strain would the months or years apart place on their marriage? And their lives in different hemispheres were both subject to the uncertainties of war.

As autumn seeped into winter Mildred began to feel the first signs of the insidious, amorphous chill of depression descending on her. Although it was easier this time to assign a cause to it, that in itself was no help. There was a sense of her familiar world disintegrating, and the possibility of happiness withering inside her.

Chapter 4

WAR: LOVE AND SEPARATION

Philip was based in London from July 1941 to February 1943. While Mildred struggled to maintain a semblance of home life without a husband, Philip could be said to have enjoyed a good war. And at some point during this time he met Clare Moilliet, who was to become an important part of his life. Not surprisingly perhaps, there is no mention of Clare in his letters to Mildred. But the letters offer some clues as to when and how they might have met.

News of the Blitz had led Philip to expect scenes of devastation in London. In his first letter of 6 July, written a few days after his arrival, he expressed his surprise to find the city apparently functioning as usual:

> … the damage is a good deal less than one would have expected to see for the scale of attack … I am certain most Australians have an entirely wrong impression of what London looks like. For instance I half expected to see the Strand a complete shambles, and places like Piccadilly Circus and Leicester Square mere rubble heaps – Oxford Street ditto. As a matter of fact the damage is surprisingly small in proportion. In the Strand there are a few odd buildings burnt out but St Mary Le Strand is not damaged at all, traffic still flows much as usual except that there are fewer private cars. That marvellous institution, the London Bus, and its driver still carry on – with women conductors mostly. In fact the amount of traffic is amazing. In Leicester Square only one corner next that Quality Inn was directly hit. Piccadilly Circus looks a bit sombre without its neon lights but is otherwise much the same.

Cinemas and theatres were open, but closing earlier at night because of the blackout. The Prom concert season, which he and Mildred had sampled in their London years, had just started, but, with the destruction of Queen's Hall, its traditional home, had moved to the Albert Hall. The loss of the historic Queen's Hall was much felt. Even sadder for Philip was the fate of the Temple Church, where his favourite organist Thalben Ball had held sway: an incendiary bomb had left it an empty shell, its interior gutted and organ destroyed. Later he would take a bus into the East End to see the worst evidence of human suffering from the Blitz.

If in the 1930s he had had somewhat mixed feelings about the English – his Anglo-Australian loyalty to the imperial cause giving way at times to irritation and annoyance with what he saw as hidebound English laziness and spinelessness – the war seemed to resolved those doubts:

> ... the most amazing thing is the way London carries on just as if nothing had happened. I wouldn't call it "grim determination" because there is nothing grim about the average Londoner. Nor is there anything suggestive of furtive fear. I suppose Kath Gordon would understand as well as anyone we know what I mean. It is a sort of typical British cheerfulness that has a capacity to ignore unpleasant things in a manner that at times amounts to an indifference which the humourless might consider idiotic. At any rate, whichever way you look at it or try to explain it, London (and the rest of the old country) simply carries on and you must admire the spirit.

It is notable that he summons up Kath Gordon, the Western Australian friend they had got to know on the *Orion*, as if the three of them had together articulated an Australian view of Britain and the English.

There had been one letter from Mildred awaiting Philip at Australia House, but in this first London letter he only gets round to mentioning having received it in the concluding paragraphs. It had been written *before* the two letters he had received in New York (which had been sent air mail) so its news was already dated. But if this earlier letter also contained the kind of reproaches which had characterised those missives, Philip studiously ignored them. His previous letter, written at sea, when he was in some danger, had revisited the affair and its legacy. Now he preferred to put that behind him, and concentrate rather on telling the story of his experience of England at war.

Before he had a chance to find permanent accommodation in London Philip was off on a ten day tour of duty, together with an offsider, Flight Lieutenant Swifte, and their WAAF driver. The British Air Ministry provided them with a large Vauxhall, and on the relatively empty roads – petrol was of course severely rationed – their experienced driver frequently touched 70 miles per hour. Passing through Andover Philip managed to say a brief hullo to surprised friends. In South Wales he and Swifte had a 'delightfully refreshing' swim – their WAAF driver presumably cooled her heels in the car – but they had a busy schedule. The summer countryside had its familiar beauty, except when scarred by defence works and balloon barrages. He was struck by the increase in cultivation, particularly of vegetables: 'everyone is becoming garden-minded'. And you could not help noticing the presence of evacuees from the cities, mostly children.

On his return to London he found a 'flatlet' in Bayswater, not far from Orsett Terrace where the family had lived in 1937-8. The landlady was 'a motherly soul' and there was 'plenty of well cooked food'. Meat, sugar and dairy products were, however, rationed, and fruit was a luxury. It was not long before he was boasting that he had successfully traded fourteen lumps of sugar for one orange.

If the country was full of evacuees, in London it was the refugees you noticed. A constant reminder of the war was the requirement that you had to have your gas mask with you when out on the street. Nevertheless London tried to maintain a semblance of normality. Two hours of daylight saving in summer enabled theatres and cinemas to stay open until a reasonable hour. Philip was pleasantly surprised to find the summer exhibition at the Royal Academy on as usual. And there was the reassuring Englishness of a Prom concert, with the legendary Sir Henry Wood, founder of the Proms, conducting before a patriotic audience. Londoners, Philip remarked, were making hay while the days were long enough.

Then on 19 July, out of the blue, he received a brief cable from Mildred advising him that she was giving up the maisonette in Nott Street and moving to Sydney.

Hearing of the recurrence of her daughter's depression, Mildred's mother Edith had come down from Sydney to offer support. After the years of hardship bringing up ten children on her own, Edith had found her circumstances improved for a time as her sons grew up and found employment. After Mildred there had been a procession of younger brothers – Jim, Doug, Noel, Jack and Ray. At the tail end of the family it seemed as if the search for names had exhausted itself. Jack was christened plain Jack, without any second name.

As the sons began to contribute to the family income, they rented a substantial house in Ryde, 'Gogaburn', which boasted a tennis court.

Surprisingly, the family seemed to weather the Depression without undue hardship; indeed, there was a sense of, if not prosperity, at least good times for the boys who, unlike their unlucky elder brother Will, had been too young to serve in the Great War, but grew up in its shadow.

But one by one the sons began to marry and move out. In the 1930s the remaining sons organised a move to a pleasant house in Manly, 'Cooeenoo', which had the kind of harbour view people took much more for granted then. For the Bragg boys the appeal of Manly lay in the modern pleasures of sand and surf and the social life associated with the beach. Described in the ferry advertisements as 'seven miles from Sydney and a thousand miles from care', Manly was a magnet for the young.

By 1941 only the youngest son, Ray, remained with Edith, and they moved into a ground-floor flat at the Queenscliff end of Manly beach. It was a bit of a come-down after 'Gogaburn' and 'Cooeenoo', and it signalled that the illusion of independence that Edith had enjoyed, with a household of sons providing a family income, was coming to an end. They now were having families of their own.

Ray had joined the Militia (what had formerly been known as the Citizen Military Forces) and was sometimes in camp or called up for guard duty. So Edith was often on her own and suggested that Mildred might like to join her in the Manly flat. Given the upheaval involved in a move it was not an easy decision to make, but it seemed that with the onset of her depression, moving to Sydney, with the presence there of the wider family, had a sense of retreating to home ground. Melbourne was tainted by Philip's affair.

Edith and Mill helped with the move. Most of the furniture and family possessions went into storage. Mildred decided that the family finances could run to keeping Barbara at Korowa as a boarder for the remainder of the year, so she only had John coming with her.

Initially, at least, it was something of a relief to be back in Sydney, with family on tap, even if the rather cramped and dingy ground-floor flat in Collingwood Street was much less commodious than the Melbourne maisonette. It was, however, just a couple of blocks away from sea and beach, and a short bus trip from Manly Wharf, from where you could take the half hour ferry trip to Circular Quay.

The Manly ferry, the main form of transport to the city, was an institution. The pride of the fleet was the *South Steyne*: built in Scotland, and claiming to be the world's largest operational steam ferry, it had gone into service in 1938. During the day passengers were serenaded by busking musicians. Of particular interest in the trip was the experience of crossing the Heads, when

Studio portrait of young Pearl, thoughtful,
perhaps also suggesting her reserved temperament.

Young Philip proudly wearing his RAAF uniform, confident direct gaze.

FLYING OFFICER P. M. RICKARD, R.A.A.F.

A caricature of Philip at the organ – an unusual accomplishment for an Air Force officer – taken from *The Navy, Army & Air-Force Journal*, 1 December, 1932. Flying Officer Rickard is described as 'socially always in the thick of things'.

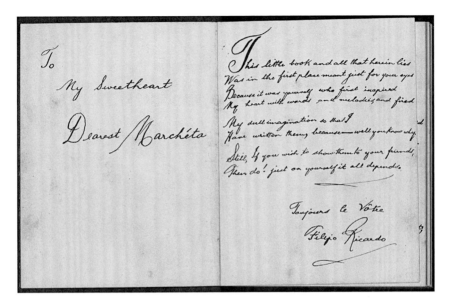

To
My Sweetheart

Dearest Marchéta

This little book and all that herein lies
Was in the first place meant just for your eyes
Because it was yourself who first inspired
My heart with words and melodies and fired
My dull imagination so that I
Have written them, because — well you know why.
Still, If you wish to show them to your friends,
Then do! just on yourself it all depends.

Toujours le Vôtre

Filipo Ricardo

The dedication page of the autograph book: Filipo and Marchéta,
the romantic beginning of the courtship.

Pearl and Philip bathing at Lane Cove,
very likely on Boxing Day 1925 when
he proposed to her. But who did they
ask to take the photo?

The newlyweds outside St Anne's church, Ryde: the sun is shining.

Pearl's wedding dress, short as fashion dictated in 1927, but oddly retaining a traditional train.

Philip dressed to attend a royal levee at St James Palace with Pearl in fur cape, probably in 1938, not the levee referred to on p.32 when Pearl was in Andover. A levee was an all male affair, though the presence of Pearl and other wives suggests that something had been organised for them. Philip was attending one of the last levees, which were discontinued after 1939. The woman on the left wearing glasses is Kath Gordon, the friend met on the *Orion* whom they saw much of in England.

Philip at the organ, totally absorbed in music. It is not clear where this photo was taken.

Tuesday 11

Fairly quiet day.
Wrote to Auntie Hilda
& Mother. Cut sandwiches
this evening in
readiness for to-morrow
We will have to arise
before 5. A.M.
Weather does not look
too promising.

Wed contd

to the balcony of the palace
after the procession was over, &
acknowledged the cheers of the
crowd. We walked up to
Piccadilly – had some early
supper, & went to a variety show
at the Windmill Theatre. There
were a few risky jokes & some
nude girls, but altogether
it was fairly entertaining.
Heard the King's broadcast
at 8. P.M. after a walk around
the West End we came home.

Wednesday 12

Early breakfast. Caught
Inner Circle train & were in
our seats by 7. A.M. Terrible
jam in the train. Our seats
were in a very good position
right opposite Buck. Palace, so
were able to see everything
going & coming back. The
pageantry of to-day was an
unforgettable sight. The uniforms
of the various regiments, together
with the mounted bands Dominion
Contingents, Indian Officers & men
in their colourful dress &
bright turbans. The Royal
family all looked their best.
The little princesses looked
very sweet. The Gold Coach
in which the King & Queen
drove is a most marvellous affair.
The greatest thrill of all was
to see the King & Queen wearing
their crowns on the return
journey from the abbey. The
Royal family came out on

Pearl's diary, 12 May 1937. Such an important event as Coronation
meant borrowing an extra half-page from the previous day!

The Presentation at Court: Philip in formal court dress, sword and all,
hired for the occasion. He knew he cut a good figure.

The Presentation at Court: Pearl, poised, elegant; one of the photographs
taken at a studio after the event, at midnight or later.

Baby John in his pram with Philip, outside 'Little Steps', their house in Andover. It would appear to be winter, but open windows suggest an Australian need for fresh air.

The Austrian maid, Maria Ruppitsch, with John, whom she took particular care of.

John on his tricycle outside the maisonette in Nott Street, East Malvern, early 1941, the photograph taken by Philip before his unhappy departure for the United States and England.

Pearl, now preferring to be known as Mildred, November 1941, possibly
taken by a street photographer at Manly, when she was on her way to catch
a ferry to Circular Quay. Why did she get a print of this sad photograph?

The happy family in Dubbo, seated on the front lawn of Buena Vista, 1943, the photograph presumably taken before the drama of Clare's letter.

Barbara and husband John emerging from St James Church Sydney after their wedding. Barbara's dress, with its floor-length, full skirt (this was the time of the Dior 'New Look') but without a train, makes an interesting comparison with Pearl's wedding dress in 1927.

Myself, early 1950s, not quite an angry young man – John Osborne's *Look Back in Anger* did not arrive on the scene until 1956 – but looking decidedly moody. Mildred has more tactfully written on the back of the snap, 'Johnny in thoughtful mood'.

Me in the foreground with Ron perched behind, holidaying on the Hawkesbury River, 1960.

Mildred's self portrait. An arresting image, a good likeness and, it seems, the only portrait she ever attempted.

The view from Philip and Mildred's Kings Cross flat, painted 1961. Through the gap between the tall apartment blocks we see the pristine, new El Alamein Fountain.

you looked out to the open sea. Usually the incoming swell would be only briefly felt; in rough weather, however, there was the excitement of the ferry seemingly at the mercy of the raging sea, the boat groaning and creaking as the windows were lashed with spray. Then suddenly you reached the calm of the inner harbour and could relax and enjoy the picturesque journey to the Quay, regally lording it over the smaller ferries that served the nearer suburbs. The half hour trip could be a bracing prelude to the pleasures of a day in town.

There was pleasure to be derived from the children. She relayed to Philip amusing titbits from Barbara's cheerful, schoolgirlish letters from Korowa, full of boarding school escapades reminiscent of *What Katy Did*. As for John, it was a relief for Mildred that the Manly primary school proved much more to his liking than the Malvern school. It may have helped that he had an aunt teaching there, though he was not in her class. (There seemed to be relatives everywhere in Sydney.) Each day, in the company of other school kids, he would walk to and from school along the mile-long beach esplanade – it was a time when no one thought twice about children walking to school. It was a cause for amusement when John tearfully confessed that one of his companions on the walk home had been blackmailing him, threatening to tell their teacher, Miss Brewer, of the disrespectful ditty John had heard in the schoolyard and had chanted in his presence:

Ooer ooer ooer!
Poor Miss Brewer,
She fell down the sewer.
They pulled the chain
And up she came
Ooer ooer ooer!

A penny a day would buy the blackmailer's silence. As Mildred pointed out to John, the threat of telling Miss Brewer about the ditty was one he was unlikely to carry out.

It was winter, so swimming was off the agenda, but Manly had its compensations. At times it seemed more like a self-contained community than a suburb. This sense of separateness distinguished it from popular Bondi which, in the public mind, was little more than a beach. Manly's hub was The Corso, the short main street (now, inevitably, a mall) linking the harbour wharf and the ocean beach with its majestic parade of Norfolk pines. The Corso had picture theatres which, while not rivalling the city's picture palaces, were nevertheless a cut above the run of the mill suburban cinemas.

Determined not to give in to the depression, Mildred sought occupation and diversion. She resumed singing lessons, enrolling with the well regarded Roland Foster at the Sydney Conservatorium. She also sat for and passed a home nursing exam, a qualification which the war might have encouraged her to seek.

But Mildred's depression did not lift; it was like a heavy cloud lowering over her consciousness. Waking from sleep, which was a kind of escape, she would slowly become aware that it was still *there*. But with the company of family and friends she was better able to cope; or so it seemed. She wrote every week to Philip, often long letters, as if this task would at least occupy her mind; she apologised for their sometimes rambling nature. It seemed as if their dialogue, fractured though it was by distance and the uncertainty of mails, was returning to something more like normal.

Philip did not learn of the onset of Mildred's depression until September, her letter having taken more than two months to reach him. He was overcome with guilt:

> This is the first you have told me about being ill, but I have been fearing to hear it ever since I left. Just when you most wanted and needed that happy companionship and its memory, I failed you and hurt you cruelly. Don't imagine I don't need that companionship too – I've missed it and wanted it more than ever since I have been away from you. It is worth more now than when we first married. I do hope for a chance to win it back when I return. But when I left Sydney in April I felt as though you didn't care much about it any longer & were probably secretly relieved to see the last of me.

And, as if responding to some concern Mildred had expressed about his well-being, he told her not to worry about him, adding miserably, 'I am not worth worrying about in any case'.

His weekly letters, fluently written with hardly a correction or a crossing out, set out to interest and amuse, conveying a vivid picture of what it was like to be living and working in war-time London. Finding satisfactory digs was an initial problem. While he conceded the food at the Bayswater establishment was still good, he had soon come to the conclusion that the landlady, far from being a 'motherly soul', was actually 'a sly money grabber', charging him for meals he wasn't having, and he suspected the maids ('Irish by the way') were reading his letters; all in all the place was full of 'too many queer people refugee Jews and stickybeaks'. There followed a rapid sequence of moves, first to Clarincarde Gardens, where the breakfasts were 'lousy' and they tried to ration hot water, then to an 'American flatlet' nearby in Linden Gardens, where he had barely unpacked when the opportunity came up to move to a superior establishment around the corner, Vincent House. It had been recommended to him on his arrival, but at that point it was full up. Vincent House was a six-floor art deco block of serviced flatlets (a term which seemed to have taken on in London); his was on the top floor, with a private bathroom, modern furnishing (which meant a 'divan' rather than a bed), central heating, electric kettle and telephone. The £3.5.0 a week charge included breakfast and one other meal per day. Two of his RAAF colleagues from Australia House were moving in at the same time, so he would have company.

Soon he had hung three little framed prints from the Wallace Collection in his room – Frans Hals' 'Laughing Cavalier', Pieter de Hooch's 'Woman Peeling Potatoes' and the Velazquez 'Lady with a Fan'. Photographs of Mildred and the children were on the bookshelf by his bed. 'What I want now to complete the decor,' he wrote, 'is an Australian scene to have on the wall above my divan: something like one of Arthur Streeton's water colours of the Hawkesbury – blue water, clean sand, clear sky and bunches of sturdy gum trees.'

At Australia House his superior was Frank McNamara, whom he knew well from his earlier time in London. Mac, as Philip always referred to him, was a sociable character, easy to get on with, though there were times when Philip would also characterise him as 'spineless'. But just as he was settling into his position, they learnt that Air Vice Marshal Williams was about to descend on them, despatched to set up and command RAAF Overseas Headquarters, which would incorporate the air liaison office, with responsibility for the increasing numbers of personnel serving in the Middle East and Europe. Williams, the son of a South Australian miner and his wife, had been a much decorated pioneer of the Australian Flying Corps in the Great War and one of the founders of the RAAF. However his subsequent career in the Force was complicated by his troubled relationship with his rival, Air Vice Marshal Goble, who had played a similar role, and who, like Williams, had issues with the way he had been treated by the politicians.

Williams had been Chief of Air Staff for the infant RAAF since 1922, but was effectively sidelined in 1939 following a report by an RAF Marshal, Sir Edward Ellington, on the organisation and efficiency of the RAAF, which was critical of his administration. Goble then briefly occupied the position of Chief of Air Staff but soon resigned, protesting that an RAF member of the Air Board had been undermining his authority. At this point Williams, with the support of the air minister James Fairbairn, was hoping to be reappointed Chief of Air Staff, but the imperial-minded Menzies decided to bring in a senior RAF officer, Air Marshall Sir Charles Burnett. Williams and Goble may have been rivals, but they had both experienced, and their careers suffered from, the Australian government's susceptibility to imperial influence. The RAF sat in judgment over the RAAF. As one historian has put it, 'the basis had been laid for the plundering of Australia's air defence resources for the benefit of Britain's war effort in Europe'.

The command of RAAF Overseas Headquarters was something in the way of a consolation prize for Williams, who came to London with a sizeable chip on his shoulder. The effect of the Ellington Report on his career was public knowledge, and Williams would not have appreciated being a subject for gossip in London. As if to spite his imagined critics, he proved a demanding taskmaster. For Philip, the new administrative structure meant that he acquired the title Senior Equipment Officer, though this was not a promotion. They worked long hours and most Saturdays, and occasionally were called in on Sundays as well.

At a personal level Philip much preferred Goble to 'Dickie', as he always referred to him. Whereas he described Goble as being 'friendly and approachable', he saw 'Dickie' as dour and humourless, a judgment, it must be said, borne out by Williams' later autobiography, uninvitingly titled, *These Are Facts: The Autobiography of Air Marshal Sir Richard Williams KBE, CB, DSO*. He was not a man to hide his light under a bushel.

As summer gave way to autumn daylight saving was phased out. Getting home on the bus in the dark was now quite a challenge. In the blackout conditions it was difficult to guess your stop, particularly as the bus windows were either boarded up or the glass pasted over with a coarse lace curtain designed to prevent splinters flying inside. There were still people sleeping in the tube stations, as they had during the Blitz of the previous year – 'a strange and moving picture of humanity'.

In spite of the demands of work Philip managed a fairly regular diet of concerts. He was often able to nip down in the lunch hour to the National Gallery for one of the famous concerts organised by Myra Hess. The Gallery interior was a strange, desolate space now, its walls stripped of their paintings, moved elsewhere for safety. And in winter he went to more than one concert in unheated halls where the orchestra were wearing topcoats.

But at summer's end the undoubted musical highlight was the last night of the Proms. Sir Henry Wood's Fantasia of British Sea Songs was already an annual feature, with the promenaders stamping the rhythm of the Sailors' Hornpipe. It was followed by 'Home Sweet Home', played as a cello solo with a harp accompaniment. 'It was all I could do to master an overwhelming desire to cry like a very small boy, it was so moving.' Over his time in London he heard Elgar's 'Enigma Variations' three times, most notably conducted by the young John Barbarolli. It was, he decided, 'without doubt my favourite orchestral work': 'it seems to traverse the whole field of human emotion and whoever is not moved almost to tears by its beauty must be a very dull unimaginative soul'. Music took on a special significance in the midst of war and separation. It provided 'escape for a while from loneliness, from the madness of these times and from a personal sense of frustration'.

He was missing his own music making. He was delighted, therefore, to be introduced to a Major Wood, retired from the Indian army, a bachelor of 82, who had a Bluthner grand piano. The major had only taken to playing the piano on his retirement, and his trembling fingers did not always hit the right notes in the Chopin prelude he attempted:

> But it was obvious that he loved his piano like a child, and that it gave him an intense satisfaction. And were my fingers itching to try it too? When my chance came, it was a thrill of pleasure to me to hear its full, clear and rich chords. What did I play first – that fine processional hymn "Ye watchers & ye holy ones" – you know the one in the English Hymnal which finishes with a row of five Alleluias – and then I played "Danny Boy" and could hear you singing it beside me.

Music was a bond between them. Hearing a contralto at the National Gallery singing the famous aria from Gluck's *Orfeo ed Eurydice*, sometimes translated as 'Thou art lost and gone forever', he was immediately reminded of Mildred singing it.

Philip followed the political situation in Australia with interest, as they all did at Australia House. Labor had made strategic gains as the 1940 election, and the anti-Labor coalition, led by Menzies, had to rely on the support of two independents to continue in office. It was perhaps politically unwise of Menzies to spend three months in early 1941 abroad, mostly in England, where Churchill invited him to sit in on the War Cabinet. On his return in May he found his United Australia Party colleagues much divided and his leadership questioned. On 29 August he resigned, and Arthur Fadden, who had been acting prime minister in his absence, formed a government. Philip thought that 'whatever Menzies' ability, there is no denying his smug brand of egoism caused friction both with his own party and with Labour people'. Fadden, he believed, was 'a far better type', but the consensus at Australia House was that his government was in danger of disintegrating like its predecessor. They were right. Fadden lasted a mere forty days as prime minister before the independents withdrew their support, and in early October Labor, led by John Curtin, took office. Philip thought it was 'about time' Labor was given a chance, but he wondered how long the new government would last.

It was when he was settling into Vincent House, and imagining how a Streeton print of the Hawkesbury would make him feel at home, that the news came through that took the war to a new level. On 7 December Japan, in a massive attack deploying over 350 aircraft, bombed the American fleet at Pearl Harbor, bringing the United States into the war. Within a few days the British HMS *Prince of Wales* and *Repulse* were sunk. Overnight Australia, as Philip put it, had been drawn to 'the edge of the vortex of the conflict':

> Although we have heard of no attempted attacks on Australia yet, all Australians here cannot help but feel anxious for the safety of our loved ones 12000 miles away in Australia. I do hope and pray for your safety. This conflict is spreading like a bushfire everywhere.

Mildred read about Pearl Harbor in the *Sydney Morning Herald* of Tuesday 9 December. The *Herald* thought there would be few Australians 'who, during the past twenty-four hours, will not have looked with new eyes upon a land suddenly grown dearer under the shadow of danger'.

Mildred and Philip had grown up at a time when Australians were increasingly aware of Japan. Ever since its emergence as a military power early in the twentieth century Japan had been the potential Asian invader in the Australian imagination. In the 1930s Japanese expansionist militarism was initially directed at China, but it was not long before its gaze focused hungrily on the natural resources of Malaya and the Dutch East Indies. Japan's entry into the war was not, therefore, entirely unexpected, but the scale of the assault on Pearl Harbor, made before any formal declaration of war, came as a profound shock. Within a few weeks – on Christmas Day in fact – Hong Kong fell. Singapore was suddenly seen as vulnerable.

It was in this context that prime minister Curtin, writing a New Year's message published in the *Melbourne Herald* of 27 December, made his dramatic 'Australia looks to America' appeal. He introduced it by remarking how 'extremely difficult' the Government had found it to make Australians realise the seriousness of the war situation. Now there was no escaping it. Britain was no longer relevant to Australia's defence. 'We know ... that Australia can go and Britain still hold on.' The nightmare of an Asian invader had, it seemed, become a reality.

January was a tense month in Australia. In Malaya the Japanese were closing in on Singapore. Closer to home, Rabaul was under attack. Curtin told Australians that 'the peril is nearer, clearer, deadlier than before'. In Sydney the trappings of war had materialised on its doorstep. At the end of the street Mildred could see the beach transformed in readiness for invasion – barbed wire stretching from one end to the other, and pits dug to impede the progress of tanks.

It was partly a response to this sense of Manly's vulnerability that led Mildred and Edith to give up the flat and move inland to a house in Gordon on the North Shore line. As Philip commented, 'Manly would be right in the front line if any attack were made on Sydney'. It was ironic that the family vacating the Gordon house were taking flight to the Blue Mountains.

But there was another reason for giving up the flat. Mildred's sister Sybil, with her two daughters, June and Noelle, was going to join forces with them, so a larger house had to be found. Barbara also was back with the family, having completed her year at Korowa. Philip's brother Bill and his wife Helen had recently had a house built in Pymble, and Mildred had visited them there. It was quite a palatial two-storey affair, with a spacious lobby dominated by an imposing staircase, and boasting what was called a breakfast room as well as a formal dining room. It might not have been to Mildred's taste, but Mildred envied the sense of suburban stability underpinned by home ownership. Bill and Helen would certainly have sung the praises of the salubrious North Shore neighbourhood, and this visit may have provided the opportunity for checking out local real estate agents.

No. 4 Yarabah Avenue was a comfortable suburban house, with a good-sized backyard. As a gesture to modernisation its California bungalow-style front balcony had been converted into a sunroom. It was in easy walking distance of the railway station, Gordon shopping centre and St John's Anglican church which, with its picturesque little graveyard, bore some resemblance to a village church. It was convenient, too, that Ravenswood Methodist Ladies College was just the other side of the Pacific Highway and was able to take Barbara.

In the crisis conditions of war this hastily assembled household took on the character of a female family reunion. It was a case of making do together as the war unfolded with alarming rapidity. Singapore fell in February; a few days later Darwin was bombed. General Macarthur, just appointed supreme commander of the allied forces in the south-west Pacific, arrived, with some fanfare, in March. The 'Yanks' started to pour in, their presence providing some measure of reassurance as the Japanese advance continued, New Guinea now at risk.

Rationing of food and clothing had been imposed, not as severe as in England but sufficient to create an atmosphere of austerity. Bread and dripping, a tasty staple of Depression days, made a comeback. Tea leaves were used twice. Cream was unavailable, and vanilla became the only flavour of ice cream.

It happened that the summer of 1941-2 was a time of drought, with Sydney's dams running low. Dust from central Australia blew over the city, rendering the sky reddish brown. At night the moon was a luminous yellow: it was grimly joked that the man in the moon had taken on an Asian appearance. On the night of 31May three Japanese midget submarines sneaked into Sydney harbour, with the intention of attacking Australian and American warships, but succeeding only in sinking a ferry which was being used as a depot ship, accommodating sailors, 21 of whom were killed. This was the only Japanese success in what was essentially a suicide mission. Two of the submarines sank in the harbour, one escaped, its whereabouts remaining unknown until its wreck was located more than sixty years later. The mission was little more than a gesture but was a cause for great excitement. The two submarines that were recovered became Sydney's war trophies.

At 4 Yarabah Avenue everyone seemed to be busy. Sybil had volunteered for the fire service, though there were jokes about what her responsibilities might be. Mildred put in time at the American canteen which catered for the young GIs who had invaded the city. She reported on their strange table manners; she was also slightly shocked by the amount of uneaten food they sometimes left on the plate. But all agreed the Americans were polite, even gentlemanly compared with Australian soldiers, and at least one niece was soon enjoying the glamour of dating one. For Mildred the busy atmosphere of the house, and the liveliness of the company, seemed to help keep the depression at bay.

A few days after the drama of the midget submarines the American navy repelled a Japanese attack on Midway Atoll, inflicting considerable damage on the Japanese navy. The Battle of Midway marked a turning point in the Pacific war. If there ever had been any real threat of a Japanese invasion of Australia it now receded. As if aware of this, the owners of 4 Yarabah Avenue, restless in their Blue Mountains hideaway, announced their impending return. Mildred and Sybil were faced with another move.

For a seven-year-old the war had a kind of comic strip reality. My mother encouraged me to write letters to my father in London which I dutifully did. I would sometimes include a drawing of an aeroplane. I think I had some awareness that he was actually *in* the war (indeed, in the plane I was drawing) while we were watching the conflict from a certain distance. He had been away for less than a year when we moved to Gordon, but I was already beginning to lose a sense of what he was like. My letters were addressed to a stranger whom I knew had something to do with me.

The midget submarines gave the war a tangible presence. On another night the siren sounded and it seemed as if the war had finally arrived at 4 Yarabah Avenue. The house did not boast an air raid shelter, and according to the drill a table was to be placed in the hall, and all of us were to squeeze in underneath it. I remember the tension as we sat there waiting, as it were, for the bombs to fall. Nothing happened. At last the all clear was heard. There was much giggling when there was difficulty extracting my grandmother from under the table.

Yet the next morning when I woke up I still somehow imagined that the landscape would bear the scars of war. I ran outside to investigate, to find, to my disappointment, that suburbia seemed to be entirely intact and undisturbed.

In one of her letters Mildred told Philip that she had come across the poems he had written for her during their courtship. If it was with an inevitable sadness that she revisited those innocent days there seemed to be no trace of bitterness. In reply Philip confessed that he had recently started to write a poem, 'To Music'. The effort, he said, made him think of those days when they had been 'so very happy together'. He asked her to be patient with him. 'I need you so. You know me.'

Philip seemed to be thinking more and more of home. One night he heard the song 'Marchéta' played on the air; he concluded his letter, 'so bye bye Marchéta – my dearest one … some especially tender kisses for yourself'. In another letter the tone was both wistful and tenderly amorous:

> I miss Ba and Johnny after the evening meal and the bit of fun and nonsense before they go to bed, then the cup of tea by our two selves, the music together and the quiet talking before bed, and then when all the house is quiet to hold you very close to me in bed and love you. There are things I miss more and want more than ever after 14 years being married to you dearest.

It was as if war and distance had made such memories more intense, more potent.

On another occasion he caught a BBC program, 'Australia Calling', which featured the evocative sound of bell birds and whip-birds, and Peter Dawson singing 'Waltzing Matilda'. But it was 'the ringing laughter' of 'the grand old kookaburras' that got to him:

> That last touch was grand to hear, but it really did give me a keen touch of home-sickness. In a flash I could see myself as a small boy – not much bigger than our Johnny is now – could see myself getting up on a summer's morning, walking outside by the fruit trees in the backyard & hearing the old "Jackies" cackling away in the tall gum trees that overlooked the top end of our allotment. Later in the day would follow the din of the locusts [cicadas] as the sun warmed things up.

These pangs of homesickness were heightened by the uncertainty of his future. For most of 1942 he had no idea of when he might be posted back to Australia. 'Dickie' Williams was a continued cause of frustration. Dickie seemed unable to delegate; according to Philip he was always calling conferences 'wasting everybody's time instead of letting us get on with our jobs. He has wasted hours & hours of my time over a period of some weeks fiddling about with shoulder badges for airmen and considering the minutest details of shape, colour and size of lettering, while I should be getting on with something important such as the supply of aircraft and engines'.

He confessed that he had 'never been so utterly fed up in my life since I joined the service'. And that was saying something. An added cause of discontent was that although MacNamara had recommended him for promotion in 1942 the Air Board was not forthcoming. Naturally he blamed Dickie, who had returned to Australia in January.

There was excitement, however, when Australia's external affairs minister, Dr HV Evatt, descended on them in May 1942; in his 'gyrations' Evatt was 'stirring up people and things generally in London'. It was a hectic but interesting week:

> Old Mac has taken me on several occasions to see the Minister to help
> him explain matters. And he is a difficult man to deal with too. However
> I think we came through O.K. And what is more important, have helped
> to get more of what Australia wants to fight and win this war.

Philip thought Curtin was 'making a good and earnest job of things' and was very dismissive of 'Menzies and his crowd'. He had little to say about British politics, though it's not surprising that he thought Churchill 'a living wonder'; he also remarked his surprise at finding himself, at the Royal Academy summer exhibition, standing next to Labour leader and deputy prime minister Clem Atlee, 'not too busy to neglect the aesthetic side of life even in these times'.

And even in war-torn England there were still opportunities, through London's imperial social network, for a colonial officer to have an occasional weekend in the country. There were the Millbournes – she was Australian – who had 'a lovely old house set in a typically English country garden – you know the sort of thing – sloping lawns and patches of flower garden bounded by a red brick wall against which are trained rambling roses and a number of apple and pear trees'. The Millbournes were lucky enough to still have a servant, 'a funny little man with a squeaky voice' – Philip thought he must have been a 'sexual freak' – who cooked and did everything for them. Such a character provided a touch of English eccentricity to the weekend.

In July 1942 he had his first taste of leave – a week on the estate of Mr and Mrs Francis Scott at Windermere, just half a mile from the lake. 'Obviously very well-to-do', the Scotts enjoyed keeping open house, and still had a full complement of servants to make this possible. He was greeted by Mrs Scott who was 'kindness personified'; while he was enjoying a cup of tea his bag was whisked upstairs to his room and its contents unpacked and neatly put away in drawers. The Scotts were patrons of the arts, particularly music, and among their guests was the composer Armstrong Gibbs. There were also three young Australian pilot officers, members of a bomber crew who had just completed their final training. Philip was pleased to report that they were 'really nice types' and 'good advertisements for Australia and the RAAF'.

Most mornings Philip played tennis with his young compatriots. There was a picnic by the lake and boating, a sunset walk around one of the 'Tarns' (miniature lakes tucked away in the hills) and a visit to Wordsworth's 'Dove Cottage' at Grassmere. In the evenings there was usually music, though 'the lads' seem to have been excused and allowed the alternative of the local pub. The music was either Armstrong Gibbs performing on the baby grand piano or classical records played on the radiogram. But one morning when Gibbs was elsewhere, Philip had a play, and Mrs Scott suddenly said 'that's a lovely touch you have, Armstrong is a gifted composer but just hasn't any touch at all'. He couldn't resist passing that on to Mildred.

On the Sunday they all went to church, the congregation swollen by a contingent of Air Training Corps boys; the vicar, who had been a pilot in the Great War, preached a sermon that was 'worth listening to'. Thus the idyllic week of English country life came to an end. Philip returned to London, while the unnamed Australian 'lads' of the bomber crew went off to do battle in the air. The war was full of such meetings and departures.

Faced with the need to vacate 4 Yarabah Avenue after a mere six months, the best that Mildred and Sybil could come up with was a disused shop which incorporated a residence. There might have been some embarrassment about living in a shop, but in the war you could make a joke of things like that. The shop itself became a rather gloomy lounge room; daylight could only penetrate if you drew back the curtain, putting yourself on view to the street through the shop window. The focus of the room was Edith's old wind-up gramophone, which had some of the records of popular songs of the 1920s and 1930s bought by the Bragg boys. Behind this room was a living area and a kitchen. A narrow staircase led to bedrooms upstairs. After the house-and-garden ambience of Yarabah Avenue the shop imposed an atmosphere of wartime austerity.

Mildred was regaining confidence in her singing – 'nerves' had sometimes been a problem – performing now and then in concerts through the agency of her teacher. Philip sent her songs that he had heard in concerts and thought would suit her voice, to add to her repertoire. Singing was always an important form of expression for her.

It was not, however, enough to ward off or overcome the insidious depression. When, with the threat of any invasion or attack receding, Sybil and her daughters moved out to reconstitute their own household, she was also left more on her own, though Edith continued to be a help, particularly with babysitting John. She had for some time been seeing a psychiatrist. She was prescribed whatever anti-depressants were available at the time, but they seemed to have little effect. There was also the mention of possible 'injections'.

There is a photograph of Mildred taken by a street photographer at this time. (Street photographers patrolled city streets during the day, taking snaps. You were handed the photographer's card and a few days later could inspect the photos at a shop counter, often in one of the city arcades, and decide whether you wanted to order any. Family albums of the time often featured some of these 'day in town' snaps.)

In this picture Mildred is on her own, well dressed in a tailored suit and hat, with gloves and handbag, the kind of ensemble required for a day in town. Yet her face is drawn, without any hint of a smile. The photographer has caught her attention as she walks along the footpath but has not been able to evoke any response. It is a look of immense sadness. And strangely, this is not the usual busy street scene; there are no figures in the background. It is a cloudy day – she is carrying an umbrella – which adds to the feeling of grey loneliness. One wonders what led her to acquire this photograph. It's almost as if she wanted it to document her unhappiness.

In November 1942 she was admitted to the Cabarisha Private Hospital at Castle Crag, the harbour suburb that had been developed by the designer of Canberra, American architect Walter Burley Griffin. The hospital had its origins in a house that had been built for the colourful Labor politician King O'Malley who was a great supporter of Griffin and his work. In 1927 it had been acquired by Dr Edward Rivett who envisaged it as 'a hospital that was more a home than an institution, in which people could be nursed back to health in an atmosphere of peace and tranquillity'. By 1943 it had been considerably extended and its gardens, which afforded harbour views, landscaped. Placing Mildred under Dr Rivett's care for a couple of weeks was clearly intended by her doctors to give her some respite from family responsibilities and cares. Perhaps, too, it included a course of supervised medication such as the 'injections' earlier referred to. There is no evidence to suggest that she underwent shock treatment, which was still in its infancy; that would come much later.

In a letter Mildred referred almost casually to her 'spell' in hospital; she had liked Dr Rivett and seemed to think Cabarisha had done her some good. But she was always reluctant to talk about what Philip called her 'nervous trouble'; perhaps, too, she did not want to burden him with her suffering when he was so far away.

I had no inkling of what my mother was going through. Apart from the 'spell' at Cabarisha she was always there for me. And she was there for others.

My closest friend at Gordon Public was Ronnie. I was a bit below average height for my age, but Ronnie, a freckle-faced kid with ginger hair, was much shorter than me. We formed an alliance and spent much time together. I knew that Ronnie's mother was ill; she seemed to be confined to her darkened bedroom. One day there was a knock on the and when Mother opened it there was little Ronnie, pale and stricken. He announced that his mother had died and burst into tears.

My mother brought him inside, sat him on her lap and consoled him. The sentiments she expressed were conventionally religious – what else could they be? – but it was the tenderness of her compassion that stayed in my mind. In her own suffering her heart went out to the little boy who was being introduced to the reality of death.

It was not surprising that Philip, a gregarious man who had grown used to the comforts of home life, should experience loneliness, holed up in his room at Vincent House. But at some point in 1942 he met Clare Moilliet and his emotional life underwent a dramatic change.

What do we know of the mysterious Clare? Alas, little more than the bare details of birth, marriage and death. She was born Dorothy Clare Snowden, the daughter of a schoolmaster and his wife, in 1905; later her father would enter holy orders. In 1928 she married Scott Trevor Moilliet (who seems usually to have been known as Trevor) at the Chapel of the Holy Trinity in Littleham cum Exmouth in Devon. Her father, the vicar, solemnised their marriage. Trevor, who was some fourteen years older than Clare, was the adopted son and only child of Charles Ernest Moilliet and Mary Francis, née Mercer, of Great Malvern, Worcestershire. Trevor had served in the

Great War, enlisting in the Army Cyclist Corp and ending the War as a Lieutenant Captain in the Worcestershire Regiment. In 1928 he gave his occupation as 'Captain (late) Worcestershire Reg. (retired)', which was tantamount to saying 'gentleman', and suggests that he was blessed with a private income. His father had died in 1923; his mother, who was a witness to the marriage, still lived in Worcestershire. Interestingly, Trevor lopped two years off his age when marrying Clare. Was he sensitive about the age difference? There is no record of the birth in England of the little girl in the photograph with Clare, which suggests that she and Trevor were living outside of England during the 1930s, in Europe, or perhaps some outpost of the Empire. Trevor went back to the Worcestershire Regiment during the Second World War, gaining the rank of Major.

Clare's name does not appear in Philip's letters, so it is not a case of Philip meeting someone at a dinner or party, someone who might have merited passing mention; a meeting which only later leads to an affair. It suggests that there was an immediate attraction when they met, and a sense of that attraction being reciprocated, so that he knew instantly to apply self censorship.

When might this meeting have occurred? Philip's wistful and erotic memory of the evening rituals of home life, with the gentle and relaxed progression to the intimacy of bed – 'double beds are so matey, aren't they?' he joked in another letter – was his most eloquent and patently sincere expression of longing for Mildred and all that she meant for him. This letter was written on 22 March. A week later another letter echoes that feeling of longing: 'I want to hold you very very close and tell you I really love you.'

But thereafter it is noticeable that, although his interesting and informative letters continue at weekly intervals, the expressions of love and affection are more formulaic and, at times, almost offhand. In May he concludes one letter with a general message – 'My love and kisses to you all, Ever your Philip'. In July he is simply 'your affectionate husband Philip'. Several times he tells Mildred to 'keep smiling' (possibly drawing on the expression 'keep smiling through' made famous in Vera Lynn's 1939 song 'We'll Meet Again'), an injunction which could well have irritated someone suffering from depression. More and more he uses some variation of the expression 'I'll ring off now' to segue into the concluding message. In one letter, written on one of his weekends in the country, he sends her 'some especially tender kisses' but signs off as 'your wandering but loving husband'; it's almost as if he's signalling that his affections might be wandering too. While, obviously, he was not going to tell Mildred about the affair, he could not, in all honesty, woo her in his letters while sexually involved with Clare. The tone remained affectionate and caring, but the erotic edge was missing.

Letters from Australia often arrived at unpredictable intervals, but it is significant that in midsummer there was a two-month period in which he received no letters at all from Mildred. Philip later calculated that ten of her letters had gone missing, presumably lost in ships sunk. One wonders whether this silencing of her voice made it easier for him psychologically to embark on the affair – and the fact that Clare was also married meant that they both faced the same dilemma. This was a 'Brief Encounter' with a difference: they may have hesitated, but the affair was definitely consummated.

Many years later Philip said that he and Clare had met through music. Clare, being the daughter of a clergyman, would, at the very least, have appreciated Philip's interest in church music. One of the churches Philip attended, which had, even in wartime conditions, maintained a reputable choir, St Mary Abbot's Kensington, he and Mildred knew from their London years. But in March he had stumbled across a nearby church, St Paul's Vicarage Gate, which he was previously unaware of; it was attached to the parish of St Mary Abbot's. The vicar of St Paul's, a bachelor, had actually invited him to dinner, which he cooked himself, being without a housekeeper in the war. In mid-April – that is to say, a month or so after his loving letter of 20 March – he learnt, through an acquaintance who knew of his passion for the organ, that the vicar would be happy to let him practise on the church's organ. He joyfully reported this to Mildred: 'I can hardly believe my luck, it seems too good to be true.' On at least one occasion he was to fill in for the church organist at the morning service.

London is a large city, but Philip and Clare were both living in the same Kensington area. Indeed, he had, amongst his earlier digs, very briefly had a flatlet in Linden Gardens almost opposite the house, Lime Court, where Clare resided. He might well have passed her in the street, even noticed her. St Mary Abbot's and St Paul's Vicarage Gate are both a mere ten minutes walk away from Lime Court and Vincent House. There are various possibilities: that, for example, Clare was in the choir at St Mary Abbot's, or that, through her father, she knew the vicar of St Paul's (which doesn't seem to have run to a choir). Could she have even been at the dinner with the vicar?

Then there was the retired Indian Army major, the proud owner of the Bluthner grand piano: a long shot maybe as a possible connection, Trevor Moilliet being in the Worcestershire Regiment, but the army connection is suggestive. And the major also lived in the same pocket of Kensington.

There are times when one senses Clare's presence. In his July holidays, just after his visit to Windermere, Philip had a week in the picturesque Cornish fishing village of Looe. He was, he told Mildred, looking for warmer weather and the chance to get some swimming, the nearer south coast beaches being closed to visitors. Although the weather was patchy he was comfortable during the day in shorts and open-necked shirt, changing into his uniform for dinner. It was, he admitted, 'a pretty quiet crowd, on the elderly side' at the private hotel, but 'among the not so olds we managed to arrange a couple of picnics'. *We.* At the very least it is ambiguous, perhaps deliberately so. Cornwall would have been a marvellous chance for the lovers to get away from London and the various subterfuges required to conduct their affair there. At Looe there was only the one major lie to be lived, one not uncommon during the war, which made all things possible – that they were husband and wife.

At the end of September Philip mentions that, taking advantage of a sunny weekend, 'two of us decided to do a hike in Epping Forest, making use of the Green Line which is to be discontinued from today in the interests of transport economy'. The implication is that the unnamed companion was someone from Vincent House; but the failure to name him arouses suspicion.

It is significant, too, that in this very same letter he announces his intention to leave Vincent House and take a room in a bed and breakfast establishment in Camden Hill Gardens. This move comes as a surprise, since he had been at Vincent House, with little to complain about, for nigh on a year and was, by this time, expressing the hope that he might be back in Australia by Christmas. It was late to be moving digs. He attributes it to a sudden decline in the standard of food at Vincent House, but the more likely explanation is that as the affair increased in intensity, and the possibility of his return to Australia began to take shape, in the precious time remaining for him and Clare he did not want his movements to and from Vincent House to be monitored by all and sundry. At Camden Hill Gardens, on the other side of Notting Hill Gate, he had distanced himself a little from the Kensington neighbourhood, though it was still within easy walking range.

Can we imagine what Clare might have been like? And what Philip might have meant for her?

In the one photograph we have it is high summer in the garden of Lime Court. Clare is wearing a short-sleeved dress which looks as though it dates from before the War. She has one arm wrapped around the fair-haired little girl seated beside her, and she is smiling encouragingly at her daughter. Clare is a slim, attractive brunette, and, if the photograph dates from 1942, she was 36. This tiny photograph would have slipped easily into Philip's wallet.

Philip, who turned 40 in 1942, was eleven years younger than her husband. We know little about her marriage, and how happy or unhappy it might have been. But given that at this time the expectation that a woman would be 'faithful' to her husband was much stronger than that applied to him – the man, after all, had license to have 'sown his wild oats' before marrying – one might surmise that for Clare there was something lacking. Philip's comparative youth, and his open-hearted Australian manner, would have made an impression. And there clearly was some immediate rapport between them. We know that she fell in love with Philip and was not afraid to express her emotions.

Lime Court does not exist now, having been replaced by a 1960s block of apartments. It was one of several Georgian houses, each with its own garden. Did the Moilliets own the house, or had it been divided into apartments? If, in Trevor's absence, Clare was living there with her small daughter – there may have been an older child at boarding school – was it in circumstances during the war that permitted of a nanny? All this raises questions about how and when the lovers got together, and suggests why a week in Looe would have been so tempting.

There are two ironic parallels between Mildred and Clare. Like Mildred, Clare had opted for her middle name. And just as music was such an important bond between Mildred and Philip, so, too, Clare's relationship with Philip was born of music.

From mid-1942 there was continuing uncertainty as to when and how Philip would be returning to Australia. At first he was led to believe that in a few months' time he would be leaving England on what was referred to as 'detached leave'; Philip thought this might mean some time in the United States on his way back. In September he learned that his bête noire, Air Vice Marshall 'Dickie' Williams, was soon to pay London a visit, and he thought this might be the catalyst for his own return.

Dickie, however, was never one to risk being frank and open in his dealings with subordinates. It seemed that, although Philip's return to Australia was on the agenda, his route and itinerary depended on Dickie making up his mind. There was talk of some duties en route in the Middle East and possibly India. In late November he was officially recalled to Australia, but the uncertainty remained; the prospect had emerged of accompanying Dickie on some returning mission, not something Philip would have relished. On 4 December he officially handed over to his successor in London, Carl Blake, which meant that until his departure he had no official duties. But with the Middle East and India still seeming the best bet he was actually buying 'tropical kit'.

In the New Year there were further delays which were entirely due, Philip believed, to Dickie's equivocation. And then, suddenly, in early February, Dickie departed, without Philip:

> The old boy – he of the bald head and the perpetually stretching neck – at long last left for Gods Own Country by air only after successive prisings like a most reluctant Sydney oyster. As soon as he went, so did his plan (now months old and stale) that I should go home via the Pyramids. His successor promptly agreed to my returning home by air.

So the reluctant oyster had been despatched, but there were still delays in organising flights. His disillusion with the service was reflected in his disappointment with his successor, whom he now saw as being 'unimaginative', a martyr to red tape, and given to 'verbal diarrhoea'.

During these final months Philip was leading a remarkable double life. In his letters to Mildred he gave vent to his frustration with the delays. He confessed his homesickness, and dutifully sent a cable to mark their fifteenth wedding anniversary. He recalled his silly mistake in nominating 31 September for their wedding. 'Bless you Mildred – I hope to make the 16th happier than any before, provided you can still put up with me. Anyhow let me have a good try.' He was looking forward to home:

> Darling, I do so very much want to be with you again (and the children) and look after you, take care of you and take the burden of responsibility and worry off your shoulders. Yes, I truly long for all those lovely things of home life that you mentioned in one of your recent letters – and I am determined to try and be as tender and considerate to you dearest as my impatient and selfish nature can possibly be.

As ever, during this apparently maddening time, he tells her about concerts and any contacts with mutual friends and acquaintances. He reports on his reading, which ranged from Goldsmith's *Vicar of Wakefield* to Galsworthy's

Forsyte Saga and Jack London's *Valley of the Moon*. And there were, of course, regular updates on war news: praise for that heroic triumvirate of leaders, Churchill, Roosevelt and Stalin, though at the same time believing that, in Churchillian mode, 'the hope of victory and a lasting peace depends on the union of all the English speaking peoples'. If the Empire had been found wanting, this was presumably the next best thing.

Yet while he was, with apparent sincerity, maintaining this homeward-bound conversation with 'my darling wifey', he was in the midst of the affair with Clare. In early December he decided to spend a few days in Oxford, which he and Mildred had briefly visited on their motoring tour, and one inevitably suspects that this was an opportunity for a brief lovers' tryst as their time was running out.

The uncertainty surrounding Philip's departure for Australia must have been unsettling for both him and Clare – though one is almost tempted to wonder whether Philip himself contributed to these delays, or, at the very least, was happy to go along with Dickie's protracted decision making in so far as it gave him more time with Clare. And yet his impatience with Dickie seems genuine enough, as does the embarrassment he expresses about acquaintances who, knowing that he had been recalled, were surprised to find that he was still in England.

He told Mildred that he had not expected to be in England for Christmas and had turned down several invitations, including one from the Scotts of Windermere. One might assume that with her child or children Clare would have commitments at Christmas. If Trevor was serving with his regiment in Britain would they have been having a small family Christmas? As it was, Philip was asked by 'some former inhabitants of Vincent House', a Mr Grant and his daughter, to join a 'waifs and strays' Christmas at their flat in Lincoln's Inn. It was a traditional English Christmas with goose (turkey being unavailable) and the trimmings, pudding, carols (Miss Grant being an accomplished pianist), and at three o'clock the King's speech ('easily the best he has made yet'). He does not mention whether he had any evening engagement: was there possibly a rendezvous with Clare?

Philip must have been in an emotional turmoil in these last months. He did look forward to something like a normal family in Australia, and perhaps a career outside the Air Force. When he remarks that 'we did have fun at Glen Iris didn't we?' it has the ring of truth. And he did miss the children – he made a point of writing letters to them. But Clare had awakened something in him. This was quite a different experience from the woman in the red coat who, whatever her attractions, was easily put aside;

he felt shame about that episode. Immersed as he was at this time in *The Forsyte Saga* one wonders whether he saw something of Irene, trapped in an unhappy marriage, in Clare.

Clare was someone he could share interests with. One assumes, as it was music that had brought them together, that she was with him at some of the concerts he attended. And after eighteen months London, even in its wartime guise, was beginning to cast its cultural spell again. He was appalled that none of his Air Force colleagues seemed to have any interest in music: 'the Average Australian is frankly a Philistine where the arts are concerned'. London and Clare were a heady mixture.

The problem, however, was that it was difficult to see any future for the affair. They were both married; they both had children; Australia was a long way away. Philip knew he was not going to jettison marriage and family; too much of himself was bound up with that. But he could not simply dismiss Clare as a wartime fling; to have done so would have cheapened their relationship. She had, in some undefined way, become important for him. At the very least they could stay in touch.

At last, in mid-February, they said their farewells and Philip departed for the United States and Australia.

Reading Philip's letters, did Mildred sense their changing emotional temperature? She would have noticed, surely, that the longing he expressed in the letters of March and April 1942, not just for home and family, but for her, had gradually become diluted into a more generalised expression of homesickness. In one of his last letters from London he wrote that 'I do hope you are feeling so very much better now and I do so look forward to being with you again': it sounded strangely muted after an absence of almost two years.

And indeed, it was not an altogether happy homecoming. Philip seemed irritable and out-of-sorts; to some extent this could be put down to his impatience with the Air Force hierarchy, particularly when he learned that he was being posted to Darwin, but in the wake of the passionate affair with Clare it must have been difficult for him to readjust to the realities of life with Mildred and the children in the strange environment of the shop at Gordon. Travelling through America this time he had been writing letters to Clare in England, full of the freshness of new love: last time his

American letters to Mildred carried the burden of guilt from the shabby episode with the woman in the red coat.

As he talked to Mildred about his time in England, what twinges of guilt did he feel about what he was not telling her?

I do not recall my father's homecoming, the moment when he walked in the door.

No, what the child in me chooses to remember is an occasion where I was the focus of attention. It must have been soon after his return, late afternoon, and my mother and I had come in to the city to meet him after work. He was in his uniform of course, and I felt rather special being attached to him, even though I was still a little wary of this stranger in our midst. We were walking along Castlereagh Street when we stopped outside the Embassy Theatre. Usually the Embassy showed British films, often thought by imperial loyalists to be a cut above the vulgar American fare which dominated Australian screens. But at this time the Embassy was showing Walt Disney's 'Bambi'. I was not to know that my father, like many adults, was quite a Disney enthusiast: 'Fantasia', with its classical music score, might have seemed exceptional, but in London he had also seen, and enjoyed, 'Dumbo'.

Father gave the impression that he had just had a marvellous idea. 'My goodness, "Bambi" is on here! Let's just see if we might be able to get tickets.'

The five o'clock session had already started and there was no queue at the box office. Father walked up to the box office and returned with a broad grin on his face. 'We're in luck!'

I couldn't believe our good fortune as we were ushered into the darkened cinema where the black and white supporting B class movie was on the screen. (For some reason the 'Mexican Spitfire', Lupez Vélez, comes to mind. Could it have been one of her movies?)

And then the technicolour magic of 'Bambi' unfolded before me. I was entranced. But what sticks in my mind is one of the songs. It is spring in the forest and Bambi becomes aware of the gentle sound of rain drops falling on the leaves. The invisible choir casts its sugary spell:

Drip drip drop little April shower
Beating a tune as you fall all around.

Drip drip drop little April shower
What can compare with your beautiful sound ...

I didn't appreciate it then, but the visit to 'Bambi' was not pure luck but a carefully orchestrated treat for me. It was the kind of role my father enjoyed playing.

Mildred, while welcoming and going along with this performance, might nevertheless have pondered the nature of Philip's commitment to restoring their relationship.

Chapter 5

DUBBO: CLARE'S LETTER

In April 1943 Philip took up the position of Area Equipment Staff Officer in the North West Australia Headquarters in Darwin, which was still recovering from the air raids of the previous year. After less than five months in the Northern Territory he was appointed Commanding Officer of the recently opened No. 6 Stores Depot at Dubbo, in the central west of New South Wales.

Dubbo might not have seemed the most attractive proposition after life in Sydney and Melbourne, but it had its compensations. After more than two years of separation and moving house it offered the prospect of a more settled existence for the reconstituted family. After the short spell in Darwin Philip had the expectation that he would now see out the War in Dubbo. And here, for the first time in his life, he would, as CO, be in charge. Yes, there would always be the Air Board, Dickie Williams and the Melbourne Air Force establishment breathing down his neck, but holding the rank of Wing Commander, soon to be promoted to Group Captain, he would have a degree of independence in running and administering a large unit. Indeed, the town was led to believe, for what it was worth, that the No. 6 Stores Depot was the largest in the southern hemisphere. There was also an army camp on the outskirts of the town, but it took second place now to the new Air Force presence. In the Dubbo community Philip would be a VIP.

'Dubbo' was popularly believed to be a Wiradjuri word meaning 'red earth', though, as is the case with many Aboriginal words casually appropriated by the invading settlers for place names, there is some dispute about the translation. The town owed its beginning to the need felt for rural law and order – a courthouse, police station and lock-up established in the 1840s forming the nucleus for the town. By 1943 it was a solid country town of about 10,000 people, a service centre for the moderately prosperous mixed farming (wool, wheat and cattle) of the district. Situated on the Macquarie River, the town had an acceptable main street, which took its name from the river, with a handsome post office complete with the standard clock tower, a Queen-Anne-style court house, a Great Western Stores department store, a respectable array of banks and a less respectable assortment of pubs. The Royal Hotel, however, passed muster, and Philip and Mildred would soon learn that it was the only establishment you would seriously consider for the occasional dinner out. Its menu was of the roast lamb and apple pie kind. There was almost certainly a Chinese café, but it would have been regarded as infra dig. There were several milk bars, the Golden Gate, which made a heroic attempt to conjure up the atmosphere of an American soda fountain, being regarded as the best. On other streets there were two picture theatres, the mildly art deco Monarch Empire, and the humbler Roxy, which, in a previous incarnation, had been the Protestant Hall. The town was particularly proud of its Olympic swimming pool, opened in 1935. Of more importance to the Rickards was the attractive, sandstone Holy Trinity Anglican church, designed by Edmund Blackett, which they would attend. Dubbo was also the headquarters of the New South Wales Bush Brotherhood, one of the distinctive Anglican communities that served the outback.

The house found for the Rickards was across the river in West Dubbo, which was little more than a scattering of houses, a garage and a general store. The house was one of a recently constructed pair of suburban-looking brick bungalows, plonked down in the middle of paddocks on a hill overlooking the town. The situation presumably inspired the house's name, 'Buena Vista'. This was said to be the last hill in the journey inland: thereafter it was an endless expanse of plain all the way to Bourke where the railway line terminated. The address was Stonehaven Avenue, named after Lord Stonehaven, governor-general from 1925 to 1931 – he had welcomed the Yorks to Melbourne in 1927 when the two planes had inauspiciously collided close to Government House – but this treeless 'avenue' was no more than a dusty track. Down by the wooden bridge – you got used to the familiar rumble of cars or trucks crossing it – there was an Aboriginal shanty town which was studiously ignored. West Dubbo must, however, have been showing some signs of growth, as a basic two-roomed public school was soon to be opened and John would be one of its first pupils.

The Rickards already knew a little about Dubbo through Mildred's sister Sybil; she and husband Sid had spent several years there when he had been town clerk. With this entrée they were quickly able to orientate themselves in the town's bourgeoisie. Bank managers were always significant figures in country towns: Mildred and Philip soon got to know the MacFarlands, the Scottish family who were living on the premises of the Bank of New South

Wales; Barbara was to be become a close friend of their daughter Fay. Les Scarff, who owned the picture theatres, and his young (second) wife Kath were a sociable pair; Les could usually see to it that you got good seats on Saturday night. Dr Buckingham, who was both a medico and a pastoralist, commanded respect in the town; he would later operate to remove Philip's tonsils – unusually, with a local anaesthetic. Then there were the Rosses (he was another doctor) with whom Philip and Mildred shared an interest in classical music: they had, for the time, quite impressive sound equipment. One chirpy presence on the Dubbo scene was a Mrs Mitchell, a diminutive widow, always known as Mitch, who had been a friend of Sybil's. She was always good for a laugh; Philip was not above flirting with her.

The squattocracy was most notably represented by the Clarks, who 'entertained' in some style on their comfortable property, Terramungamine. George was part of the family associated with the Sydney department store Marcus Clark's. Thelma's lively, theatrical manner, combined with her wealth, helped give her an image which was positively racy by Dubbo standards. Either George or Thelma boasted some illegitimate royal connection, through Edward VII's notorious womanising; when 'God Save the King' was played Thelma would chip in with 'Stand up for cousins!' So it was not long before the Rickards found themselves in the swim of the town's regulated social life.

'Buena Vista' was a house of its era. Red brick with a tiled roof, it had no pretensions to architecture. Its front garden had a hardy buffalo grass lawn and little in the way of shrubs. A flight of steps led up to a small balcony and the front door. The narrow hall opened onto a living room and dining room on the left, and on the right the master bedroom, opening through an archway onto a wired-in sleep-out, exposed to the elements with canvas blinds to pull down in bad weather (sleep-outs were considered healthy, particularly for children). The hall led to the kitchen, soon to be dominated by a kerosene fridge, which was sometimes given to smoking. (One of my father's chores was filling the kerosene tank under the fridge. I can see him, even now, crouched on a stool, rhythmically syphoning the aromatic kerosene from a can between his legs.)

The kitchen led to an 'L'-shaped verandah. West Dubbo was not sewered, but the house had an outside lavatory equipped with a mysterious unit called a Hygeia Dissolvenator. This Australian-designed system comprised a toilet pan mounted on a cylindrical tank. Lifting the lid operated a geared mechanism which rotated the pan, transferring whatever had been deposited on it into the tank. Caustic crystals were to be added each week, so that the resulting sterile solution could be discharged into the soil. That at least was the theory of it. It had the advantage of not requiring a weekly visit from the dunny man. The Hygeia was sometimes known as the chocolate wheel, though not in the Rickard household.

This modest house was an improvement on the shop at Gordon, and the family soon settled in. John would occupy the sleep-out, while Barbara had an improvised bedroom at one end of the back verandah. It was not long before the household was made complete by the acquisition, through the agency of Dr Buckingham, of a dog, a bright-eyed kelpie puppy who was christened Rusty. Although a sheepdog by breeding, he had had no contact with sheep when he came to us. It was, however, in his genes. Sheep would sometimes be quartered in a neighbouring paddock when on route to some destination. (Which was? The abbatoir? The railway station? I never thought to ask.) At the mere whiff of sheep Rusty felt the call. He would leap the fence and, without anyone to direct him, round up the sheep, efficiently and repetitively moving them on from one end of the paddock to the other.

It seemed as if, in this welcoming country-town atmosphere, Philip and Mildred, creating a home again and sharing the experience of making new friends, had a sense of starting again. Mildred's depression seemed to have passed. There is a photograph of the family, seated on the grass in front of 'Buena Vista'. It is high summer: Philip, Mildred, Barbara and John, all in short sleeves and sporting big smiles, look the picture of health and happiness.

And then, after Christmas, the mood was shattered.

Mildred found a recent letter from Clare – which Philip had carelessly left in a pocket, or buried under clothes in a drawer. It was a lover's letter, infused with physical passion. It was a blow of course, re-opening old wounds, perhaps even confirming a lingering suspicion; but Mildred, by temperament reserved, also found the expression and tone of the letter immensely distasteful. This was not *her* language or her way of expressing emotion. That Philip responded to it made him more of a stranger to her.

Some memories visit us through a haze, the edges blurred by the passage of time, the action sometimes almost in slow motion. But now and then a memory has an urgency that seems to cast it in the present, as if it is happening again and again in compulsive repetition.

It is after dinner. (I have no memory of the meal or the strained silence that must have dominated it.) I come into the kitchen, but stop in the doorway because I immediately sense a drama is being played out, a drama that excludes me. Father is at the sink methodically washing up, so his back is towards me, as it is to my mother who is drying up, tea towel in one hand. She is saying something to him, which I cannot hear, but he seems to be ignoring her, his eyes deliberately fixed on the work of the dishmop in his hand.

Suddenly she attacks him, grasping him by the shoulders and jumping up and down, then collapsing into tears. I am shocked by the violence of her action, so unlike her. But almost immediately I realise it is an illusion: she has, in frustration, simply been trying to get his attention.

My father becomes aware that I have witnessed this scene. My mother, still sobbing, hardly notices me.

'Mummy's not feeling very well,' he says, as if this explains what I have seen, and guides her to the bedroom.

Barbara did not witness this scene, but was close at hand. Father must have returned to the kitchen and stoically resumed the washing up, for Barbara recalls taking up the tea towel and drying the knives and forks – and suddenly her blood running cold at the nightmarish thought that our father might be planning to kill us.

On the other hand I have a memory, perhaps from the next day, when Father was at the Depot, of her comforting our mother and saying 'I am sure Daddy loves you,' though Barbara can't confirm that. It is that moment of horror with the knives and forks that stays in her mind.

I was a mere watcher, unable to offer comfort.

And a listener.

The logic of my occupying the sleep-out was that, as an eight-year-old, I would be going to bed relatively early, and would be asleep by the time my parents retired.

And that was usually the case. But that night I am awakened by voices in the dark. They are, even in the midst of this drama, still sharing the same bed. I hear my mother's anguished voice and the word 'divorce' mentioned. The name 'Clare' is uttered into the darkness, lodging in my mind. I lie there in silence, miserably taking all this in, even if I don't fully understand what 'divorce' means.

I drifted off to sleep again, but I doubt they got much sleep that night.

I have a more shadowy memory of my mother with a letter in her hand, one that she had written, in an envelope ready to post. For some reason I believed this to be a letter to Clare. It was as if she was deliberating whether to send it. She had, of course, taken careful note of Clare's address, which she had written on a small piece of paper, folding it around the tiny photograph of Clare and later placing it with Father's war-time letters. Had that photograph been enclosed in the letter from Clare which was the cause of the drama? And had my mother kept Clare's letter in her possession? If divorce was an option, the letter would have been evidence of infidelity.

And did she post her letter to Clare?

Our mother decided to take Barbara and me to Sydney. Father must have driven us to the station. Perhaps, for us, they maintained some fiction that we were just going to have a bit of a holiday, in which Father was unable to join us. I remember the overnight train journey. We had sleepers, and in those days the New South Wales sleeping cars had an almost Victorian ornateness. I think I enjoyed the novelty of going to bed on a train. The trip was an adventure, even though I dimly appreciated its seriousness.

In Sydney we went to stay with Uncle Jim and Aunty Enid in West Ryde: family could be called upon in crises such as this. Jim, Mother's younger brother, had always been her favourite. Growing up, she had been his protector in that noisy household. Now he would play that role for her. Jim was a kind, gentle man, with a wry sense of humour; he had a secure job with a bank. Enid, the daughter of an Anglican clergyman, was a wiry woman, bossy but loyal, with a firm sense of values.

I remember nothing of this stay. It is not clear on what terms Philip and Mildred – I will still need to refer to them in this way from time to time – parted. One assumes she just wanted time to think things over. The woman in the red coat had tarnished the marriage and inevitably affected the way she regarded him: it had been a cause for disappointment but not divorce. But Clare was another matter. Clare's relationship with Philip seemed to go to the foundations of their marriage.

One consequence of this escape to Sydney was that the news of the crisis in the Rickard marriage inevitably spread around the family. The affair with the woman in the red coat had been kept fairly quiet, but Philip's relationship with Clare was soon common knowledge in the Bragg and Rickard families.

Was Mildred seriously considering divorce? Or was she expecting some peacemaking gesture from Philip? If so, the letter which eventually came from Dubbo was not entirely a surprise:

Dubbo,

13th January 1944

Dear Tiddles,

For the sake of Barbara and John's happiness and future I am prepared to have another try to keep our home together. If you feel equal to it and can bear to live with me, I'll promise to stop corresponding with Clare. I won't ask anything of you except that you do not taunt me with my past actions. You know I would work hard to make you all as comfortable and happy as possible.

Please let me know as soon as possible Tiddles, as this state of suspense is getting unbearable.

I am truly sorry to have hurt you so cruelly – telling the truth so often seems to hurt, and that was why I tried to hide these things from you. Please give my love to Ba and John.

Yours affectionately

Philip

It is a carefully considered, austere letter. If they are to reunite it would be for the sake of the children. He promises to stop writing to Clare, but in return asks that Mildred not 'taunt' him with his infidelity. But while he is 'truly sorry' to have hurt her he is not apologising for the affair. He is not making excuses; there is no suggestion that this was just a wartime fling, a consequence of loneliness and frustration. And in so far as he is prepared to give up Clare – or, at least, to give up writing to her – there is an ultimate bleakness about the letter. There remains a sense in which he is not capable of 'giving up' Clare, of forgetting about her.

And yet this message is bound up in the intimacy of their marriage relationship. He does not write, as in most of his London letters, to 'Dear Mildred'. He uses the nickname 'Tiddles' which, as a kind of shared joke, each used for the other. There is an implied appeal for mercy. The 'state of suspense' is unbearable. Their marriage may be damaged, and he has to accept the blame for that, but he can't live without it and the warmth and comfort of family life.

If Mildred did give serious thought to divorce it was a daunting proposition in 1944. Divorce court proceedings were targeted by the gutter press. *Truth*, the sleazy weekly founded by the notorious Ezra Norton, took particular delight in reporting the sometimes lurid detail of these cases. It was a form of public humiliation for 'guilty' and 'innocent' alike.

A phone call must have been made. We returned to Dubbo. I have no memory of the journey home.

Back in my sleep-out, on a warm summer night I am awakened by voices again. But this is not a conversation in the ordinary sense. I hear my father's voice addressing my mother in breathless, halting tone. It sounds as if he is lying on his back. From my mother there is only a wordless murmur.

What is happening? I am mystified but also disturbed and alienated. I think about getting up, to investigate, but that seems out of the question. I lie there, paralysed, buried in the pillow.

Raising my head again and listening for any clues, I register the sound of bodies rearranging themselves. A kind of silence has returned. I am brave enough now to get up and turn on the light. They are lying on their backs, close to each other, and look up at me with some surprise and concern. What's the matter, my father asks.

I look at them accusingly. 'I want a glass of water.'

I go to the kitchen and return to my bed with the water. Nothing more is said.

When Philip wrote, 'I won't ask anything of you', it implied that he would not necessarily expect a resumption of sexual relations. But of course returning to 'Buena Vista' meant returning to the double bed which was, as he had once said, 'so matey'.

My 'primal scene' – the term Freudians apply to such childhood memories, whether real, imagined or repressed – made no sense to me at the time, and partly for that reason was troubling; it was not something I could share with anyone.

But years later, realising what I had witnessed in the dark, I came to see it as evidence of reconciliation. I cannot, if pressed, be entirely sure that this 'scene' took place *after* the showdown about Clare, but that is where my memory has chosen to locate it.

And, indeed, from my childhood perspective, family life seemed to resume, as if the whole drama of Clare had been something we had imagined.

A couple of weeks after our return to Dubbo I fronted up to the new but humble West Dubbo public school, a standard two-roomed temporary timber structure in a barren paddock; here the main social distinction was between those who wore shoes and those who came barefoot. Our teacher, Mr Whiteley, had been gassed in the Great War, and had been attracted to Dubbo because of its dry, healthy climate. Mr Whiteley saw to the planting of a row of pepper trees along the boundary, which we kids were required to water with buckets.

In the classroom each row of desks represented a separate form. The standard was not high, and after my arrival I was soon promoted to the next row, virtually skipping a year. One night at dinner I said casually, summoning up all my acquired sang-froid, 'Pass the bloody salt'. My parents looked at each other in a sadly knowing way; clearly West Dubbo Public was a bit rough. They were very protective of my rather English accent, which was something of an embarrassment for me, particularly in the West Dubbo schoolyard.

I developed a great interest in weather and weather records; indeed I was an authority on the average annual rainfall of every major country town in New South Wales. Dubbo turned on some interesting phenomena for the would-be meteorologist. In summer a red-coloured dust storm might blow in, and perched on its hill 'Buena Vista' was exposed to its attack. One year there was a plague of locusts. Trying to walk through the enveloping cloud of these air-born creatures was an eerie experience. Another time, after heavy rain, the river rose dramatically; I waited excitedly for it to break its banks and cut us off from the town and was disappointed when denied the flood.

In 1946 I graduated to Dubbo High School. On the first day of school my father, in full uniform, accompanied me, checking me in, I suppose, at the school office. I was mortified to be led by him through the noisy asphalt yard, which, with the assembled throng watching our progress, had the atmosphere of a colosseum. Father subsequently arranged for a RAAF driver to pick me up each morning in a jeep and deliver me to school, a further cause for embarrassment. I used to ask the driver to drop me around the corner to minimise the chances of my privileged taxi service being observed.

Philip and Mildred were soon back in the demanding whirl of country-town social life, in which they were leaders. This busy calendar, and the behaviour required of it, may well have served to take their minds off the family drama. If news of Philip's affair had spread around the family network in Sydney, in Dubbo it was a well kept secret.

Every church (with the possible exception of the Methodists) and every organisation in the town seemed to have a ball; and of course the Officers' Mess at the Stores' Depot had also become important in the town's social life. There were picnics, parties, dinners. Philip and Mildred were responsible for suggesting a progressive dinner party, in which each course was enjoyed at a different home, something they had been introduced to in England. The party, rather noisy by this stage, culminated in dessert at Buena Vista.

There wasn't much in the way of theatre in the town, but there was a determined group known as the Dubbo Merrymakers. Mildred sang in one of their concerts. She wore the dress made for her Presentation at Buckingham Palace, but struck by nerves, felt that she had not given of her best. Not that the audience noticed.

As the war drew to a close Philip was increasingly looking to the future, the old restlessness returning. In 1945 a confidential report, required, it seemed, at regular intervals for all commissioned officers, was made by Group-Captain Harold Seekamp on Philip's record as CO of the No.6 Stores Depot. In the section 'Appearance and Bearing', Seekamp ticked 'Most impressive, Stands out among his fellows'; he also praised his resourcefulness and leadership qualities. However in the section 'Emotional Stability' he placed his tick against 'Somewhat moody and capricious'. And while Rickard was a good organiser who 'gets things done well' his proficiency in 'the discharge of his duties' was only average. The catch was that while he was 'a very capable equipment officer' who displayed 'ample initiative' he held 'very decided opinions of his own' and was 'inclined sometimes to question the wisdom of directions from higher authority'. It had a familiar ring. Philip was probably irritated that Seekamp, holding the same rank as himself, had received an OBE (Military Division) in the 1945 New Year's Honours List. It would have confirmed his suspicion that Seekamp was not one to question 'the wisdom of directions from higher authority'.

Anzac Day had a particular importance during the war. It fell to Group Captain Rickard to lead the Dubbo march. With his impressive 'appearance and bearing' he looked good at the head of a march. He was a visible presence in the town. Mildred, as his consort, had her social responsibilities which included graciously opening a fete now and then. Indeed, the Rickards seemed to have an almost vice-regal aura in Dubbo.

Some time at war's end Philip's elder brother Bill paid a visit to Dubbo. The partnership he had formed in 1926 with his friend Varco Jones was now a small, successful engineering business. Jones was on the verge of retiring: he was very much the business half of the partnership, while Bill was the engineer. Bill, a dour, gruff man, was impressed by Philip's managerial skills in running a large establishment like the stores depot, which, in addition to its RAAF staff, had come to employ 200 civilians. As a result of this visit Bill suggested that Philip might like to consider joining the firm, taking over Varco Jones' position. There was also the thought that it might be appropriate now for the partnership to make the transition to a private company.

Philip was attracted to the idea. This seemed to offer a very satisfactory escape from the frustrations and irritations of service life. There was just one hitch. If he completed twenty years with the RAAF he would become eligible for a pension when leaving the force. This would mean staying on till the end of 1946. It is not clear whether it was pressure from Bill to join the firm sooner rather than later, or whether it was Philip's impetuosity, that led him to opt for demobilisation on 18 July 1946, less than six months short of gaining the pension, which would have been a useful financial contribution to the Rickards' budget in the postwar years, when they were struggling to set up house in a climate of inflation and shortages.

Dubbo turned on an impressive farewell and presentation, presided over by the Mayor, to mark Philip's departure: the Dubbo *Dispatch* described it as 'the largest and most representative gathering of citizens yet held in Dubbo'. The Mayor said that while carrying out his work at the Depot in a very efficient manner, Group Captain Rickard had proved himself 'a sterling citizen', always ready to give advice and assistance. The Honourable George Bassett, a member of the New South Wales Legislative Council, made a point of acknowledging that Philip was 'blessed with a very good partner as wife to help him, and she had endeared herself to the people of Dubbo'. He was sure Group Captain Rickard would be 'just as successful in business as he had done for the country'[sic].

In accepting the silver tray and set of six silver mugs, an 'attractive and interesting gift which was something after his own heart', Philip could not resist making clear his reasons for leaving the RAAF. 'He did not think the Air Force was progressing in the way it should, and he could not see any way of influencing opinion himself'. He reminisced that when he had gone before a selection committee in 1926 he had been 'the first post-war no.1 applicant'. 'It was easy to get in but hard to get out.' His most interesting experience in running the Depot had been his 'contact with civilian employees and ordinary working men'. He had enjoyed his work for the community and would take away from the town valued friendships. He also made a point of thanking the representatives of the airmen, sergeants' mess and officers' mess for their support. He seems to have been well liked by those working for him.

If the Melbourne Air Board establishment had got wind of the sentiments expressed about the Force by Philip, it would have confirmed for them the verdict of Seekamp that Rickard was 'inclined sometimes to question the wisdom of directions from higher authority'. He would now be one of the many being demobilised and returning to the community, except in his case it was after almost twenty years of service life.

It might have seemed with the end of the war and Philip about to start a new career at Jones & Rickard that Clare had receded into the past. But there was a legacy. Edith found it hard to forgive him for the unhappiness he had caused her daughter. This sentiment was shared by others such as Enid, who had experienced the drama at first hand. Mildred was popular in the family: no one had a bad word to say about her. Philip's good humour and charm would not necessarily wash with them.

And then there were the children. They had been witnesses; they knew.

Yes, *we* knew and remembered.

And what about Clare? How did all of this affect her? Was she able to return to her marriage after the war as if nothing had happened? And do we know if Philip kept his promise to stop writing to her?

Almost fifty years later I revisited the site of the drama. 'On my way to Dubbo and the 1940s,' I wrote in my diary, as I set out from Melbourne in 1992.

DUBBO: CLARE'S LETTER

I approached the town from Parkes, driving along the Newell Highway, which took me past the Western Plains Zoo, a branch of Sydney's Taronga Zoo which occupies the site of the old army camp, and was now Dubbo's main tourist attraction. (In 1944 no one considered the possibility of tourists.) The highway brought me directly into West Dubbo, which was unrecognisable, totally suburbanised, thick with houses as well as a couple of motels. Yet, in the absence of familiar landmarks, I almost instinctively turned left and found myself at the West Dubbo Public School. Not surprisingly, given the surrounding development, it too had been transformed, now an odd assortment of buildings colliding with each other. All that survived from 1944 were the pepper trees we had planted and watered, now gnarled and stately, offering plentiful shade to our successors. I introduced myself at the School Office and paid my respects to the board with the names of the principals, Mr Whiteley, 1944–57, heading the list.

Leaving my car at the school I crossed the highway, camera in hand, and walked the short distance down what was now a street to Buena Vista, on the corner of Stonehaven Avenue, a corner which did not exist as such in 1944. The two houses were still there, but now encased in suburbia, not an empty block to be seen.

Nevertheless Buena Vista itself seemed little changed, though the front garden now had a recently planted solitary gum tree. I paused to take photographs and noticed that the front door was ajar. I walked up the steps to the balcony and became aware of the sad drone of television from within. I tapped on the door and a yawning, long-haired youth answered the knock. I explained, with some self-consciousness, that I had lived in this house as a child. Would he mind if I took a look inside? 'Go ahead, mate,' he said, not showing much interest in the history on his doorstep, and, ushering me in, retreated into the living room on the left where he returned to the thrall of daytime soap opera, which he was watching with two other youths, presumably co-tenants and possibly unemployed. The rooms, of course, seemed pokier than I had remembered. I walked into the main bedroom, looking out into the sleep-out, now glassed in with louver windows but otherwise unchanged. I paused there, trying to block out the sound of the television, as if I might still recapture traces of my parents' voices lingering in the air.

And then the kitchen. And here I am taken aback, because the layout is not as I remember it. In my memory the sink was in front of the window which faced onto the verandah, and I was positioned in the doorway from the central hall, witnessing the scene on a diagonal angle. But here the sink is on the left. There is no suggestion of the kitchen having been modernised; the space is smaller than I recall, 'positively tiny' I wrote in my diary.

So where precisely was I? I try to re-enact the scene, pressing the 'Pause' button at particular moments. Perhaps I am already in the kitchen on the far side from the sink, and my parents, aware of my presence, are keeping their voices down, which is why I can't hear what they are saying. But suddenly the tension is too much for my mother and she 'attacks' him.

That is plausible. But memory has its own laws and resists correction. And even if I am unsettled by the reality of the kitchen, in my mind I know what I saw. I was there.

Chapter 6

ST IVES: THE FAMILY UNIT

A chink of tea-cups pushed aside
and we fall silent.
That time of many conversations
is long gone. We tried hard
to shed reserve,
you dying, I still hoping
you were not...

— Barbara Fisher

Sydney in 1946 was a hectic place. Thousands of soldiers were being demobilised; many had married during the war and were already starting families. The war economy had seen an end to the unemployment of the 1930s, and Labor's program of postwar reconstruction was dedicated to maintaining full employment and creating the prosperity which would banish the hardship of the inter-war years. But the problem was that, in the short term, the economy could not deliver the goods and services which people were beginning to demand. House building had stopped during the war: now there was a huge leeway to make up. And building materials were in short supply. Accommodation was desperately difficult to find.

Philip and Mildred were helped out by relatives. (In one sense that was what was expected of relatives then.) Cec, the brother-in-law of elder brother Bill, and his wife Nita, had a holiday house on Burraneer Bay, Port Hacking, the southern edge of Sydney. They made this available to the Rickard family – for a suitable rent presumably. The house, at the bottom of a steep hill, was on the water, with its own tidal swimming pool and a rowing boat. It boasted a billiard table, which also doubled as a dining room table. So for a time the illusion was created that the family were enjoying an extended holiday.

Relatives visited at weekends. Port Hacking at the foot of the garden offered the kind of scenery that could be described as pure Sydney.

But it *was* a holiday house, with a basic kitchen and a chip water heater for the shower. There wasn't much in the way of heating. And it was hardly convenient. A bus took you to Carringbah, a station on the Cronulla line. And Cec and Nita would sometimes come down at weekends, so that there was the feeling that we were living in their house under sufferance.

Philip had not needed a car in Dubbo; that was provided for him. Cars were also much in demand after the war, but somehow a modest Morris 8 tourer was acquired. This little sardine tin of a car bore humble comparison with the stately Dodge driven by Philip's brother Bill. We were the poor end of the family in a dependent relationship with Bill and Helen: it was Bill who had brought Philip into what now resembled a family firm, and it was through Helen's relatives that we had a roof over our heads.

It went without saying that Philip and Mildred shared the postwar dream of having a house of their own. Through twenty years of married life they had been constantly on the move – indeed, Mildred could count eleven rented houses or flats she had lived in during that time. Now that Philip had thrown off the shackles of the ordered Air Force existence they could look forward to living in one place, without the threat of periodic uprooting.

A block of land was bought at St Ives, then a semi-rural outpost of the desirable North Shore line. An almost village-like settlement of orchards and market gardens, St Ives was clustered around the road that connected the North Shore suburbs with the northern beaches, stretching from Mona Vale to Sydney's premier beach resort, Palm Beach. Acquiring a block of land was one thing: getting a house built on it was a much more difficult proposition. An architect, Adrian Ashton, who had designed brother Bill's two-storey house at Pymble, was engaged. Because of the shortage of building materials a house could not exceed 12½ squares, a size which would seem ridiculously small for a young couple with children today. Ashton produced a compact, if unimaginative, design for a three-bedroom house. But it was clear that translating this design into bricks and mortar was going to take time and patience.

Cec and Nita were showing signs of irritation with the Rickards' continued occupation of their beach house. Another move was deemed necessary and a bleak little house at Dee Why was rented for a few months before something better was found in Queenscliff – half of a down-at-heel timber house built into the side of a steep hill (the kitchen window looked into a cliff face); however the living room commanded a splendid view of the long arc of beach stretching down to Manly. This was at least familiar territory for Mildred from the time spent in her mother's flat during the war.

Through this disjointed time Philip would jokingly speak of Mildred as 'a hausfrau without a haus'. This phrase became part of family lore, so much so that Mildred acquired a family nickname of 'Frau'. Barbara and John would soon discard the 'Mummy' of childhood years and address their mother as 'Frau'. The 'haus' that beckoned like a vision on the distant horizon was the dwelling depicted in the architect's drawings, destined to be 14 Benaroon Avenue, St Ives. As the pain and drama of Clare dissipated with the years this house represented the promise for the future. The quest for these 12½ squares of suburban security could be seen as Philip fulfilling the commitment he had made to provide for Mildred and the children. And as her part of the contract Mildred would be the 'hausfrau' who would dutifully, and indeed lovingly, create the ambience of a happy home. But in characterising Mildred as a housewife Philip was also recognising that they were no longer the lovers of old.

Because of the uncertainties of house and home, I was, after a grim term at Sutherland Intermediate High, boarded at Knox Grammar for a year. I only encountered the Dee Why house in school holidays when its main attraction for me was not the nearby beach but the Seagull Library, one of those small commercial lending libraries that was to be found in every suburban shopping centre. There I discovered Agatha Christie and began systematically to work my way along the shelf filled with those quintessentially English murders. Agatha's whodunits were set in the middle-class, home-county world my parents had encountered in England.

I had more experience of the Queenscliff house, which we were still inhabiting when my year as a boarder was completed. Here, one Saturday afternoon, my father, in a rather deliberate manner, suggested a walk, just the two of us. This was such an unusual idea that I should have realised something was up. Father paused at some point on the walk, as if to enjoy the view, and we sat down on a rocky outcrop, whereupon he began to tell me about something called 'the facts of life'. What was all this leading to? I wondered. 'Soon you'll get interested in girls,' he explained. Somehow this struck me as not only a faintly indecent suggestion, but also as distinctly unlikely. I think we were both embarrassed by this conversation, and I'm not sure what he made of my guarded reaction.

Slowly, laboriously, the house was built. The foundations laid, there was a long pause before bricks and bricklayers could be obtained. Months went by. There were regular visits to monitor the halting progress. When the four of us were packed into the little Morris 8 Father instituted a family ritual which jokingly celebrated that we were a tightly knit little family. As the drive began he would call out, as a military command, 'Family Unit, Numbers! One!' and we would respond, in turn, playing the game, 'Two!' 'Three!' 'Four!'

Benaroon Avenue was a new street with only one or two houses, and we had the feeling of being pioneers on the frontier of suburbia. At last this agonising process gave birth to a house which at least made a virtue of its modest dimensions, unlike the pretentious, sprawling villas which were later to create a new brand of suburbia. Its oblong shape allowed for a driveway down the side to the usual separate garage at the back. The brick walls were cement rendered and painted white. The architecture made a gesture to Georgian order and restraint, a style which Philip and Mildred had learned to appreciate in England, and which was beginning to be recognised as part of the Australian colonial inheritance. The Georgian windows facing the street had green shutters which, never in fact being shut, were for appearance's sake. Window boxes added a dash of colour.

Inside the house had its modern features. Mildred had longed for the soft, quiet opulence of wall-to-wall carpet, and her wish was granted in tastefully muted green. In the living room there were white bookshelves, built into the wall. Here many of the books acquired in their English years would take pride of place. A narrow hall led to a master bedroom and two smaller bedrooms, all within easy reach of the compact bathroom, with the shower in the bath, and a separate lavatory. The bedrooms had the innovation of built-in cupboards, removing the need for cumbersome, old fashioned wardrobes. The living room, with its couch and armchairs fitted with loose covers and the piano in one corner, led to the dining room which opened onto a walled terrace overlooking the backyard. Years later this terrace, which lacked the shelter provided by a verandah and was not much used, would be glassed in and become a sun room. The kitchen was just large enough to allow for a small central table, a throwback to the traditional kitchen, though its patterned laminex surface pointed to the future. The kitchen accessed a back porch and a small laundry with an electric copper and wash tubs. Later a primitive washing machine known as a 'Trayway', which was basically an electrically operated agitator fitted onto one of the tubs, would be acquired. The backyard, which fell away down the side of a hill, was dominated by a tomb-like septic tank. A willow tree planted nearby grew with miraculous speed. It would be many years before St Ives was sewered.

After the makeshift accommodation of the last two years this house, small though it was, seemed the height of luxury. (But it would be several years before a phone was connected, another example of the disruption to services which was a legacy of the war.) The marriage entered a new phase, and, encouraged by the growing sense of postwar prosperity and stability, of which the modest home at 14 Benaroon Avenue was a symbol, it seemed as if an understanding had been reached that there would be no more dramas. Or at least, no dramas like that occasioned by Clare's letter.

The pubs still closed at six o'clock, which was the hour for 'tea' in most Australian homes. We regarded ourselves as rather superior in that we had 'dinner' at seven, often begun, at least, with the ABC News in the background. Before dinner there would be sherry and music. The sherry was something that had been cemented as a pre-dinner ritual during Philip and Mildred's English years. The music was in the hands of Philip at the piano. Mildred would be called from the kitchen for a song or two. It might be anything from Mozart's 'Alleluia' to a song by Elgar, Philip's favourite composer, such as his beautiful setting of Tennyson's 'Now sleeps the crimson petal, now the white'. (As a boy soprano – there had been a hope at one stage that I might have been enrolled at the St Andrew's Cathedral choir school – my repertoire was limited, but I could manage a presentable 'Oh for the wings of a dove'. Later, when my voice broke, I would be encouraged to take singing lessons. Music was part of the family culture.)

A radiogram was acquired, actually made by one of the handy foremen at Jones and Rickard, and it took pride of place in the dining room. Sunday night was dominated by the radio during and after supper. The ABC had close links with the BBC, and the most popular program on a Sunday was a half hour of English comedy. For some years it was 'ITMA' (It's That Man Again) with Tommy Handley and a gallery of characters, most of whom had a signature line which listeners waited for, such as the unhappy Mona Lot, who always concluded her sad story for the week with the doleful 'It's being so cheerful that keeps me going'. 'ITMA' gave way to a distinctively English program which we thought rather more sophisticated, 'Much Binding in the Marsh' with Richard Murdoch and Kenneth Horne, set in a run-down RAF station, which had a particular appeal for Philip. Among the minor players was Maurice Denham, one of whose characters was the affably stupid Dudley Davenport, whose signature line was, after a significant pause on realising that he had goofed again, 'Oh I say, I am a fool!' The mere utterance of this line would produce gales of laughter from the studio audience, and indeed from us at home. There was nothing 'canned' about audience reactions then. Even more famous, however, was its successor, 'Take it From Here' because, along with 'Professor' Jimmy Edwards, its two other stars were the Australians Dick Bentley and Joy Nicholls. A favourite moment was always the latest instalment of the stultifyingly boring suburban couple, the Glums; Ron and Eth were played by Bentley and Nicholls (later June Whitfield), Bentley using a broad Australian accent to comic effect. That's all an Australian accent was good for in those days.

Although the ABC did much to stimulate Australian cultural life, the British inheritance was a haunting presence. At four o'clock every afternoon the chimes of Big Ben introduced the BBC News, which emerged from our radio sets on a wave of ghostly static, a daily reminder of the distance which separated us from the land still known as 'Home'. And in the field of religious broadcasts the Church of England seemed to have a privileged position – but then, it did have the largest number of nominal adherents. Once a week in the late afternoon Evensong would be broadcast from an Anglican cathedral, usually St Andrew's, Sydney or St Paul's, Melbourne, introduced by the holier-than-thou chant of the precentor, 'O Lord, open thou our lips'; I associate that distinctly Anglican sound with the St Ives house. (It was not until 1962 that the Australian Anglican church gained formal autonomy under the title, the Church of England in Australia, and almost another twenty years before it became the Anglican Church of Australia.)

'Christ's Church militant here in earth', as the Prayer Book put it, had a less than militant presence in St Ives. The Church of England was repre-sented by a small, makeshift hall, an outpost of St Swithun's Pymble. Lay readers took Evening Prayer every Sunday, but the Rector, a well-meaning but uninspiring man, came once a month to dispense Holy Communion at 8am. Watching him taking the sacrament at the northern end of the Holy Table, as required by puritan tradition, we saw him in profile, calling to mind those Tudor images in English churches, and as he partook of the bread and wine we thought he bore a passing resemblance to a lizard, and unkindly nicknamed him 'Liz'. The Sydney diocese had for many years been controlled by the Evangelicals, and while Mildred and Philip would not have thought to complain about this when they were growing up – that was simply the church as they encountered it in Ryde – their years in England, where they had gained an appreciation of the rich diversity of the Church of England, equipped them with a more critical view. The term 'altar', with its connotations of sacrifice, was taboo in Sydney, and a cross in a church, which might encourage idolatry, was also dubious. Philip made an issue of the absence of this basic Christian symbol, and 'Liz' finally agreed to a simple cross being placed at the east end.

The music at Christ Church St Ives (as this little hall was known) was also an issue. A very basic harmonium was in the hands of the elderly, very deaf Mrs Chase, occasionally assisted by her dutiful daughter, the latter having the nickname 'Ilka' bestowed upon her by us (Ilka Chase being an American actress and writer with a particularly racy reputation, and therefore quite inappropriate for our Miss Chase). Philip could hardly contain his agony as Mrs Chase's arthritic fingers murdered the hymns. When she finally retired Philip took over, supervised the purchase of a much more sophisticated harmonium, and founded a choir. Mildred led the sopranos. The hall was extended and, with a surpliced choir, services acquired the character of mainstream Anglican worship. The Church of England, if not on the march in St Ives, was at least coming to terms with the burgeoning suburbia at its doors. And the Rickards were pillars of this new community. But occasionally, just for a change, the family would pay a visit to St James King Street, with its dignified High Church worship, or, more exotically, Christ Church St Laurence, to savour the 'smells and bells' – and music – of Sydney's Anglo-Catholic headquarters.

At a more material level, the ties with Britain in the postwar period were expressed in the 'Food for Britain' campaign. Food rationing and 'austerity' continued in financially-strapped Britain until the early 1950s. Philip and Mildred regularly sent food parcels to their English friends: tins of ham, pineapple and bright yellow peaches, dried fruits, perhaps a bottle of not-too-dry sherry. Most of these friends they would never see again.

In 1952 King George VI died. Twenty-five years earlier as the Duke of York he had been welcomed to Melbourne on the day when two of the fly-over planes had collided before his very eyes, provoking that pithy comment, 'Two of your buggers down'. Following his unexpected ascent to the throne in the wake of his elder brother's abdication, 'Bertie', as he was known in his family, struggled with a stammer to develop a regal presence in the age of radio, but, with the considerable help of his determinedly charming wife Elizabeth, and, as we now know, the Australian speech therapist Lionel Logue, he had won the respect of his people when, during the hardships of war, they were felt to have shared the experience of their fellow-Londoners.

George VI's death was big news in Australia too. 'THE KING IS DEAD' the newspaper banner headline, spread across the page, proclaimed. And for Philip and Mildred he had been part of their imperial story. They had listened on the wireless to the funeral of Bertie's father, George V, soon after their arrival in England in 1936, and witnessed the ensuing drama of the Abdication; they had watched in wonder the choreographed majesty of George VI's coronation procession; and they had, so to speak, rubbed shoulders with the King and Queen at Mildred's Presentation. They had also, in the pages of newspapers and the *Australian Women's Weekly*, followed with interest, as most Australians had, the story of the two royal children, Elizabeth and Margaret, as they reached maturity, and now the ritual sadness of the King's death was offset by the romance of the young Queen ascending the throne. Two years later she would, with her handsome young husband the Duke of Edinburgh, make the remarkable national tour when Australians, in their millions, embraced the monarchy as their own.

The English connection was important in the development of Australian cultural life after the war. The appointment in 1947 of the distinguished English conductor and composer, Eugene Goossens, as conductor of the Sydney Symphony Orchestra, signalled the beginning of a new era for the ABC's state orchestras. Goossens was a persistent advocate of the need for a performing arts centre, and is said to have suggested Bennelong Point as the site for an opera house. Philip and Mildred were among the many who became Sydney Symphony subscribers. Bill and Helen, who also subscribed, would call in their Rover, and the Rickard party would drive to the Town Hall together, though Bill and Helen, who had been subscribing for longer, had rather better seats in the gallery. Much as Philip appreciated his elder brother bringing him into the firm, Bill's comparative wealth rankled at times.

The taste for theatre, opera and ballet that Philip and Mildred had developed in England began to find scope in Sydney. In 1948 the British Council sponsored the celebrated tour of the Old Vic Company, led by Laurence Olivier and Vivien Leigh, both of whom had the added box office advantage of being Hollywood stars. The tour was designed to help reestablish the British cultural connection after the dislocation of war, and

Australians responded enthusiastically. Olivier and Leigh were accorded a reception akin to royalty wherever they went. Philip and Mildred, taking Barbara with them (I must have been deemed too young to justify the additional expense), went to see Sheridan's 'The School for Scandal' and came home in raptures. A year later the Shakespeare Memorial Theatre flew in, the first time air flight had been used to bring an entire company to Australia (the Old Vic players had made the traditional leisurely sea voyage). The Stratford company, led by Anthony Quayle and Diana Wynyard, again with the backing of the British Council, lacked the glamour attaching to the Olivier-Leigh team, but nevertheless with the prestige of Stratford reinforced the sense of English dramatic standards being set that Australian theatre was not equipped to match. (And this time I did make it to 'Much Ado About Nothing' and was suitably awed.)

Commercial theatre in Australia – which in effect meant JC Williamson, the Tivoli Circuit and Garnet Carroll – tended to confine itself to musicals, variety and the occasional proven West End play, still likely to be a drawing room comedy in which the leading lady made an 'entrance' through the French windows, perhaps with a basket of flowers from the garden, to the expected welcoming applause. But there was a struggling alternative theatre which attempted to put on the plays which the commercial managements almost automatically overlooked, and the formidable Doris Fitton's Independent Theatre at North Sydney was one such outpost; Philip and Mildred would sample its wares from time to time. It might be an American classic such as Eugene O'Neill's 'Mourning Becomes Electra', perhaps a racy French comedy by Jean Anouilh's ('Ring Round the Moon' was a favourite) or occasionally something really avant-garde such as Pirandello's 'Six Characters in Search for an Author'. Professional actors, working for a pittance, would usually take the principal roles with amateurs or students (the Independent ran acting classes) in support. There was a certain musty glamour attaching to the Independent – or so it seemed then – giving one a sense of putting a foot in another cultural world. You could even get a cup of coffee in the interval, which was almost unheard of in Australian theatres. Doris herself was an imposing presence, quite often making an appearance at the end of a performance – a distinguished actress herself she now confined herself mostly to directing plays – seeking contributions for the Theatre, which was regularly threatened with financial collapse.

Ray Lawler's 'Summer of the Seventeenth Doll', first performed in Melbourne in 1955, is always cited as signalling the beginning of a new era in Australian theatre. But part of the aura which the play acquired derived from it being taken up by Laurence Olivier and successfully staged in the West End. 'The Doll' had the imperial imprimatur.

As we settled into life at St Ives my own future began to take shape. The dislocations of war, followed by the sense of Dubbo exile, now gave way to the comfortable security of North Shore suburbia. The Rickard family connection was crucial in getting me enrolled at Knox – Bill and Helen's two sons had been to the school. Knox, founded in 1924 to educate the sons of the well-to-do Presbyterians of the North Shore, was a relative newcomer to the ranks of Sydney's independent schools. Unfortunately in my time the school was in the hands of a dour headmaster, Dr Bryden, with limited cultural interests, his two passions being cadets and rugby, both of which were compulsory. Theatre was regarded with puritan disdain, and a military pipe band flourished while the school orchestra had all but died out by the time I was a senior. Latin dropped out of the school curriculum; indeed, the only language available after the Intermediate Certificate was French, and that was taught by the History teacher who was not a linguist.

My parents wanted me to go to university; indeed my father hoped that I might be an engineer, which had been his own ambition as child, and which became impossible with the collapse of family fortunes during and after the Great War. I was sadly to disappoint him in this respect. (He conceded the point with good grace.) A university education had not really been considered for Barbara. Her being short-sighted was seen as a reason for avoiding study, while an aptitude for art was seized upon as offering a career opportunity, so that she left school after the Intermediate Certificate and, while we were at Dubbo, was sent to the art school of the East Sydney Technical College, boarding with Philip's brother Jack and his kind and mildly eccentric wife Mary. That the art school might expose her to the temptations of Sydney bohemia did not seem a concern, though perhaps Jack and Mary were seen as providing a moral anchor.

I was, therefore, something of the white-haired boy in the family, particularly when I began to win school prizes which seemed to augur well for my academic future. I was, when necessary, a bit of a swot, and, in spite of Knox's mediocre academic reputation at this time, with the aid of the two or three good teachers on its staff I saw the path to university (which meant Sydney University) unfolding before me. And through these years I grew up firmly believing that I was part of a happy, even enlightened, family. Our sense of belonging to a unique family unit was sustained by much banter and teasing and, in my case, the creation of characters whom I would 'play' for family amusement, most notably one Roy, who was a cheerfully innocent but utterly boring dinkum Aussie. There were arguments too , mostly involving Philip, with Mildred usually the mediating influence. But these arguments could themselves be given the humorous treatment and be contained within the family cosiness. So, on one occasion in a high-pitched row between Father and Barbara, he was, in his frustration with her, momentarily at a loss for words. Finally, he spat out, 'You impudent young chit of a girl!' There was a brief silence as we took this in: where on earth had that expression come from? Then we all burst out laughing, immediately defusing the tension. 'How lucky I am to have such a nice family!' I wrote in the diary which, at fifteen, I had started to keep. It was as though the memory of Clare and the Dubbo crisis had been buried, almost beyond recall.

Although history was already my passion, at university I committed myself to Arts-Law, in the interests of career, as I never for a moment imagined one could aspire to be a historian, and I shared a snobbish distaste for school teaching. While I did well enough in my Arts subjects, I found Law, particularly as taught in the Law School outpost in the city, tedious and alienating. It was a marvellous piece of luck, therefore, that, in spite of lacking an honours degree, I was runner-up for a Shell arts scholarship to Oxford, and the Company decided, as a kind of consolation prize, to send me to Oxford for a year; the not so hidden agenda being to lure me into an executive career with Shell.

My parents were delighted that I was to have this experience of England, indeed, in a form more exalted than their own immersion in RAF life in Hampshire and London. They had visited the hallowed halls of Oxford as tourists; I would actually be living and studying there. I was in awe of the whole cultural and intellectual edifice of Oxford; but also dismayed by the onset of the Suez Crisis soon after my arrival in 1956, when prime minister Anthony Eden, in league with France, orchestrated an Israeli attack on Egypt, giving Britain and France the excuse to intervene to 'separate' the warring parties and seize control of the Suez Canal, which had been nationalised by Egypt. This almost nostalgic reassertion of British imperial pride, immediately disowned by the United States, had the drunken hearties of Oxford singing 'Land of hope and glory' on street corners, but ended in national humiliation. Back in Australia my father followed 'British-to-the-bootstraps' prime minister Robert Menzies in supporting Britain against the world-wide tide of disapproval. I wrote back, in rather superior, measured tones, arguing that Britain's ill-considered intervention had resulted in precisely what it had sought to avoid, namely, Egypt rendering the Canal impassable, and thus cutting off the life-line to what was left of the Empire.

But I certainly absorbed much of the Oxford atmosphere, irritated by being benevolently patronised as a 'colonial' – and Balliol was used to playing host to outsider groups such as scholars from Scotland and America as well as the colonies – but appreciating that it did exempt me from the sometimes cruel strictures of the British class system. And at the end of the academic year I joined the Balliol Players on a summer tour in an updated version, with skiffle music accompaniment, of Aristophanes' 'The Frogs'. In this irreverent production it was decided that Euripides should be played as a gum-chewing cross between Marlon Brando and James Dean, and lacking, as it happened, an American in the cast, an Australian was seen as the best candidate for this demanding role. I threw myself into the part, mumbling and writhing in a pastiche of method acting, and, as my confidence grew, inserting contemporary references to 'unAthenian activities' and the need for 'an agonising reappraisal', the expression popularised by President Eisenhower's secretary of state, J Foster Dulles. This high-spirited, ram-shackle but privileged production was performed in the gardens of various stately homes and public schools, culminating in a performance in the Middle Temple in London. This bore impressive comparison with my parents' experience of weekends in country houses, but with more than a whiff of Evelyn Waugh thrown in. However, given my colonial innocence and reserved temperament, perhaps inherited from my mother, I missed out on the decadence of that milieu, much to my later regret.

It is notable that in 1958 when my time in England was up I decided to return to Australia via America. Was I influenced by my father's stories of his war-time travels across the United States? Perhaps, but there was also the lure of Broadway – I was a devotee of the American musical, and this was the era of two of the greatest of that genre, 'My Fair Lady' and 'West Side Story' – not to mention the lure of the The South, to a large extent engendered by the blinkered fiction of 'Gone With the Wind'. From New York and Washington I headed south in a Greyhound bus, registering the shock when we had crossed the Mason-Dixon line of realising that black passengers had obediently gone to the back of the bus. Atlanta bore little resemblance to the images thrown up by 'Gone With the Wind'; New Orleans seemed more authentic, and it was with a thrill of recognition that I saw a streetcar heading for Desire. I crossed Texas half asleep, pausing in New Mexico to be impressed by the Grand Canyon, and when, still in a kind of Greyhound coma, I made it to Los Angeles, my priority, courtesy of Evelyn Waugh's *The Loved One*, was to visit the Forest Lawn Cemetery. Satirically enjoying the syrupy ambience of the place, I saw 'The Crucifixion', a painting unveiled like a Cinerama film in a theatre, and introduced with a respectful commentary; it is still claimed to be 'the largest framed mounted to canvas painting in the world'. I was to dine out on my experience afterwards of shopping for postcards in the visitors' centre and being asked by a beaming assistant, 'And did you enjoy The Crucifixion?' San Francisco offered the more cerebral experience of hearing the Modern Jazz Quartet in a dimly lit basement bar, and then, before I knew it, I was on the *Orcades* heading home to Sydney, with my stories to tell of England and Oxford, with a dash of America seen through Anglo-Australian eyes.

The 'family unit' had already undergone a major change in 1952 with Barbara's marriage to the young architect, John Fisher. St James King Street was chosen for the wedding: it was a dignified Anglican affair with a boys' choir providing an angelic chorus. The reception was at the nearby Pickwick Club, a Sydney institution long since vanished. Within a few months the couple departed for England where John Fisher had earlier worked and established himself in a London firm which welcomed an infusion of colonial new blood. They were to spend four years in England, enjoying London life, Barbara eventually gaining a position as a copywriter with J Walter Thompson.

A month or so after the wedding Mildred, who had never enjoyed robust health, fell ill. She was experiencing palpitations which kept her awake at night. Two doctors, one a heart specialist, had difficulty in making a diagnosis and conveniently concluded that it was 'of nervous origin'. Drugs, principally digitalis (a drug, dating back to the eighteenth century, originally derived from foxgloves) brought the heart palpitations under control, but left her feeling 'drugged' and, alarmingly, she began to feel the symptoms of the depression which she had been free of for almost ten years. The drugs available at this time could do little to ameliorate it; it was little consolation that it was now diagnosed as 'cyclical depression'. It was difficult for her to describe how she felt, except to say it was like an impenetrable black cloud hovering over her (one thinks of Les Murray's 'black dog' at his heels). The floods of terrible, desperate tears that would sometimes engulf her broke down the reserve which, from her youth, she had, perhaps without even thinking about it, cultivated. The tears offered some physical relief, but were chilling in their despair. As months passed, and the black cloud persisted, shock treatment was recommended. It seemed to be all that doctors were left with when drugs had failed.

Did the shock treatment, in erasing, for a time at least, some recent memories, do any good? It was unnerving for the family visiting her in hospital that her personality seemed to have been thrown out of gear: her voice was high pitched, as if she had lost access to its natural register, and her handwriting spidery, lacking its usual ordered style. These effects were short-lived as she regained her sense of self. But, for better or worse, the shock treatment seemed more a dramatic distraction than any sort of 'circuit-breaker' cure. The black cloud was not so easily dispersed.

There was never a total collapse; always she managed to keep going. When, a year after the onset of the depression, she was hospitalised again, it was to do with her physical health. Her illness was now diagnosed as a rheumatic condition stemming from the childhood experience of rheumatic fever, which had left her with a damaged heart. The doctors never seemed to make any connection between the legacy of rheumatic fever and the cyclical depression which had plagued her since her youth.

During this difficult time Mildred, encouraged by Barbara, started doing a little painting, hoping that this would relax her. She took to it, and later, with an English neighbour friend, Edna, enrolled at the Julian Ashton Art School which was situated at The Rocks and which at this time was still being run by the kindly Henry Gibbons who had succeeded its founder Ashton. Edna, who bore absolutely no resemblance to Barry Humphries' Edna about to be unleashed on an unsuspecting Australia, was a gentle person, slightly fey in manner. One always felt there was an element of polite surprise in finding herself marooned in Australian suburbia. Mildred and Edna were a little daunted by the School, which boasted among its former students Elioth Gruner, George Lambert and Thea Proctor and, in the more recent past, William Dobell, Jean Bellette, John Passmore and Joshua Smith. But they soon warmed to the place and began to look forward to the time spent cocooned in its warm, creative environment.

Apart from the still lifes which, along with the life classes, seemed a basic part of the training, Mildred painted the scenes around her – it might be the front garden at 14 Benaroon Avenue, already dominated by a claret ash, or perhaps an autumnal Mount Wilson in the Blue Mountains, encountered on a picnic. In 1956, when her depression had long since passed, she painted a self portrait: it is a good likeness and an arresting image, the lips bearing the merest hint of a smile beginning, but the hazel eyes suggesting a knowledge of suffering. She gained some satisfaction from this exercise, and one senses it was a voyage of self discovery. She and a friend at the School – not Edna –decided, almost as a mutual dare, to submit their self portraits in Sydney's often controversial Archibald Prize. Perhaps Henry Gibbons, as a boost to their self esteem, encouraged them to do so. Of course they would have been surprised if their paintings had even been hung in the exhibition, but the two mature-age students enjoyed it as a shared adventure. She told only Philip about the Archibald Prize submission, holding him to a vow of silence, and was embarrassed when he could not help spreading the word around. But painting had become part of her life.

Barbara and her John had returned from England shortly before I left for Oxford in 1956. While I was away I wrote a weekly letter home, just as my father had during the war, and I also wrote, more intermittently, to Barbara. Writing letters was part of our family discipline, and we looked forward to receiving them, taking particular pleasure in getting one of those plump airmail envelopes crammed with half a dozen pages or more. For us the slim blue aerogrammes or air letters, which you purchased from the post office, were only acceptable as interim missives. In these letters we addressed each other by our family nicknames. Our mother was still 'Frau' and Barbara, I think, had given 'Dad' and 'Daddy' a new twist by calling him 'Dadso' which caught on.

In one of her letters Barbara took me into her confidence. In the years Barbara and husband John had spent in England, in the course of which his career had blossomed, they had increasingly felt parental pressure for them to return to Australia. This was never spelt out, but every time their return was delayed they were conscious of great disappointment at home. 'As it happened we could not help feeling ourselves a little the prisoners of family affection,' she wrote. 'Have you noticed, in our family we seldom talk about things that really matter to us?'

In another letter she cast a discerning eye over our parents:

> Dadso has an extremely dominating personality – it's only since I have been away that I realise how much I was dominated at home – in the nicest way, of course, but still I was. I felt, when we came home, that Frau & Dadso seemed a little unaware of the fact that you were an adult

too. Did that strike you? Dadso as a character baffles me. I sometimes
wonder where his real self is, he discloses so little. He is affectionate,
dreadfully sentimental, generous, but rarely, one feels, <u>natural.</u> He also
has pretty awful manners, hasn't he? Only talks when he can hold the
floor, if not, he relapses into silence. Real conversation with Dadso,
much as I love him (because I do in spite of his faults) is rather difficult.
Frau is a darling but the famous Frau reserve is, of course, there....
These reflections are rather sad. I think they are part of maturity &
everyone feels this way at some time or another. When we most need
our parents they are bound to fail us, try they ever so hard. And when
they most need us, <u>we</u> fail them'

Initially I was rather taken aback by this family analysis – it was not something
I was used to. But it encouraged me to reflect on my own membership of the
'family unit' that I had taken so much for granted. And from the distance
of Oxford I began the slow process of seeing 'Frau' and 'Dadso' as people
('Mildred' and 'Philip', almost like characters in a novel) and not just as
parents.

On my return from Oxford in 1958 I was put to work in Shell's Sydney
office. It was good to have an income, but I knew that an executive career
with an oil company was not for me. The question, however, remained what
was? I had, for a few years, been having singing lessons, even managing to
make time for them with a respected teacher in London. But now I decided,
encouraged by my 'success' in the Balliol 'Frogs', to make a more deliberate
venture into theatre, initially just for my own amusement and relief from
the tedium of Shell, enrolling for classes at the Independent Theatre with
Doris Fitton and, later, the Shakespearean actor John Alden. As a student
you were likely to be conscripted by Doris to carry a spear or play a servant
in a production, but my aim soon became to graduate from the acting classes
to what was known as Workshop, a more or less self-governing young group
which met on Saturdays and was supposed to serve as the creative engine of
the Theatre. Workshop also provided most of the talent for the children's
productions which the Theatre staged.

Even before I had been admitted to the sacred circle of Workshop, John
Alden, staging a production of 'Titus Andronicus', which was a prelude to
forming his second Shakespearean company, gave me a small part with a
couple of lines; and, indeed, at one point I think I did carry a spear. Alden's
choice of the not often performed 'Titus Andronicus' was inspired by the

recent success of Olivier's production in London, which, as it happened, I had seen.

Suddenly I was in a cast led by some of Sydney's leading professional actors, who were remarkably tolerant of us relatively inexperienced extras who were helping fill up the stage. But it was the backstage dressing-room life that provided my real education. The Independent had only two dressing rooms, one male, one female. In the crowded men's dressing room the conversation was, to use that old fashioned word, camp, full of bitchy humour and sexual innuendo. The straight actors entered into this as much as anyone else. It soon became clear to me that in the world of theatre there were few secrets about sexual orientation (though of course that term was not in use then). Homosexual actors might be 'in the closet' in the public world, but they were usually 'out' in the dressing room. Those whose sexual identity was not known were often the subject for speculation and gossip. I was probably in this last category, at least during the season of 'Titus Andronicus'.

I had been aware of my own homosexuality for some years but had difficulty in articulating it; it was something I could only hint at in the diary I had been keeping since the age of fifteen. While the knowledge that there were others like me, who seemed comfortable with their sexuality, offered a measure of reassurance, it did not, in itself, overcome my sexual shyness. Though not conventionally devout I struggled with my religion and it was a constraining influence. This was a time when, although the 1957 Wolfenden Report in England signalled the beginning of a reevaluation of homosexuality, the churches still regarded it as akin to a disease and inherently sinful. And influenced by my upbringing, I regarded casual sex as, if not blatantly immoral, certainly distasteful. So, amusing as the dressing room chatter might have been, it did not persuade me to cheerfully adopt the common practices of the homosexual subculture.

However, in Workshop I met Ron, some five years older than me, a schoolteacher with ambitions to be a theatre director. We shared interests in literature and music – he introduced me to the early operas of Benjamin Britten, most notably 'The Turn of the Screw', and that ravishing song cycle, not well known then, Berlioz's 'Les nuits d'été'. Ron had a bed-sitting room in a crumbling block of flats at Kirribilli, which boasted a superb view of the harbour and Circular Quay. The tram depot on Bennelong Point had just been demolished to make way for the Opera House, but many of the old warehouse buildings of Circular Quay still afforded suitable sites for neon signs, so at night there was a blaze of rippling colour across the water. In this shabby but romantic setting we became friends but Ron, perhaps sensing contradictory messages emanating from me, was very circumspect. When my family rented a holiday house in Avalon in the summer I invited Ron down one day, so he met my parents (the only time in fact).

Ron and I were also, by this time, part of a group, which included Jane and Sheila and Norman; Ron, all of thirty and the oldest and most experienced, was a point of reference for us. After Workshop on a Saturday afternoon there would be rowdy, convivial sessions at the pub. (Six o'clock closing had ended in 1955.) I began to appreciate that Ron was attractive to others as well as me. In this heady, new environment it dawned on me that I was in love. Ron finally took the initiative – I, of course, being quite unable to make a move – and the friendship was suddenly an affair. So in 1960, after the long, agonising journey from puberty, I had, at the age of 25, crossed the border into the freedom of strange new territory. In a sonnet, addressed to Ron, I spoke of 'my anxious happiness'. Considering this new future was a daunting prospect.

My parents had already noticed that my social life had undergone a radical change as I was spending more and more time at the Independent. Having risen in the ranks of Workshop I graduated from extra to actor in several plays which always involved long night rehearsals, the only time, apart from weekends, the cast could be assembled, and as opening night drew closer the rehearsals went later and later. But the affair meant that I was spending whatever other spare time I had at Kirribilli. I was conscious of leading a double life, but felt powerless to do anything about it. Drinks after a Saturday night performance were compulsory, and now there were the urgent demands of sex as well. I was still teaching at our local St Ives Sunday School and would sometimes front up with a throbbing hangover from the night before. And, foolishly, one night I stayed out all night without making the obligatory phone call.

My mother sensed what had happened. She remembered Ron coming down to Avalon, and, although that visit took place months before the affair had started, it seemed that even then she recognised that there was something different about our friendship.

My mother and father are framed in the doorway to my room. I see them now, holding each other, joined in their anxiety. They seem to be leaning forward a little, yet careful not to step into my room, as if somehow respecting my privacy even while intruding on it.

I am having an early night – Ron is away in the country, visiting relatives – and I am sitting up in bed, a book in hand, but hardly able to read it, such is the tumult inside me. It's as if I knew this was about to happen, and I know immediately what it is they want to talk about.

I am not able, fifty years later, to put the actual words into their mouths. There is no authorial tape recorder in my bedroom. I would not dare, in this case at least, to invent the dialogue. But the image of them, poised in the doorway, my mother's face etched with worry, my father deeply embarrassed, speaks to me across the years.

My secret I realise is no secret. Do I tell them I am in love? Do I use those words? I know that in seeking to assure them of the reality of this love I struggle for some sort of historical precedent, as if to validate my experience, and my mother intimates with a shrug of disdain, that, oh yes, she has heard all that about the Greeks.

Mention is made of the possibility of my going to a psychiatrist. I quickly dismiss the suggestion, as if it were an insult, and perhaps they, too, have doubts about it, as it is never raised again.

Later, as if acknowledging in some way the truth of my sexuality, my mother speaks of the virtues of companionate marriage. But that, for me, is mere evasion, if not deception.

It is an impasse. In my determination to defend my love I feel separated from my parents, suddenly detached, as it were, from the tightly-knit family in which I have grown up. The space between us, between the doorway and my bed, opens like a void.

It only occurred to me years later that my mother's raising of the possibility of companionate marriage could be seen as a comment on her own position. Her marriage was not companionate in the sense that she and my father ceased to have sexual relations: the double bed still presided over their bedroom. But the shabby business of the woman in the red coat could not help but tarnish the romance of their relationship, while the much more serious affair with Clare undermined the mutual trust upon which their marriage rested. Yet, given their backgrounds and the sense of duty they shared, they stayed together and made the best of things. Much of this was for the sake of us, the children, and their dealings with us as we grew up brought them together and renewed their sense of common purpose. So my image of them, framed in the doorway, was an image of their marriage, 33 years after they had, before the altar, made the solemn pledge 'till death us do part'.

Of course I was too wrapped up in the emotional whirl of my own drama to make any such observation. And Ron being away, there was no one I could confide in. I didn't have the phone number of the aunt he was staying with; but I had an address and I sent a telegram conveying, in a sentence or two, the gist of what had happened. Ron cabled back, 'I'm glad and proud'.

It may seem surprising that up to this time the possibility of leaving home and living on my own, or indeed sharing a flat with a friend, had never occurred to me. I had, soon on my return from Oxford, bought a Morris Minor on hire purchase; that was the extent of my independence. But now I felt impelled to act; it became almost a point of honour. Ron moved out of his small Kirribilli bed-sitting room and we took a larger flatette in nearby Neutral Bay. But this sudden transition to living together – ironically occasioned by my parents, in contemporary parlance, 'outing' me – was complicated by the fact that Ron had already made plans to go to England at the end of the year, which was just a few months off. I quickly committed myself to joining him, both of us with vague hopes of pursuing our careers in theatre.

Although there was this element of drama in my leaving home there was never anything resembling a break between my parents and myself. I visited St Ives regularly when we would still go through the ritual of some songs, along with the sherry, before dinner. They came to see the plays I was in at the Independent. That sad discussion in my bedroom was never resumed. Even as the date of my departure for England loomed we behaved as if nothing had happened. Ron, however, never accompanied me to St Ives, and I don't think the possibility of such an invitation was ever aired. At that time none of us would have been comfortable with it. Reading our subsequent correspondence – I wrote as regularly as I had from Oxford – you would have no idea of the drama which had preceded my departure.

The 'Neptunia', on which we were booked, was due to leave Sydney on Christmas Eve. I decided to spend Christmas with the family and fly down to Melbourne on Boxing Day to join the ship there. So on Christmas Eve I went down to the ship where many of our Independent friends came to see us off, the familiar Australian ritual; except that I then returned to 14 Benaroon Avenue.

We kept up the pretence of family togetherness on Christmas Day, but even having made the gesture of spending this all important Day at home I felt that I had cast a shadow over it. The next morning there was a tearful farewell at the airport.

In Melbourne I met up with Ron. 'West Side Story', which I had seen on Broadway in 1958, had just opened at the Princess Theatre. The ship was not departing till the next day, and we had no difficulty in getting tickets in the upper circle for the musical; in fact 'West Side Story', which took the American musical into new territory, was thought to be a bit too advanced for Melbourne, which was much more comfortable with the stylish Englishness of 'My Fair Lady'. Seeing 'West Side Story' for the second time I could not help reflecting that in those two intervening years my life had changed utterly. And the world of theatre might be thought to have been at least partly responsible.

While I was at Oxford there had been some talk of my mother making a trip to England but it remained only an idea; now a booking was made on a freighter departing in May, a cabin on a cargo ship being cheaper than first class on a liner. The ostensible reason for Philip not joining Mildred was that he was not due for long service leave until 1966, a surprising consideration, given that Jones & Rickard was essentially a family firm in which one would not have thought he would feel beholden to such rules. But as the date of departure grew nearer Mildred had a recurrence of the heart palpitations and there were fears of the depression returning. She began to worry about the trip, and the possible loneliness of the journey with so few passengers was a concern: the booking was cancelled.

Philip and Mildred were, of course, now alone in the St Ives house and, with the cancellation, or at least postponement, of Mildred's trip, the decision was made to take the opportunity for a change of environment. They would let 14 Benaroon Avenue for six months and take a flat close to the city. Their first thought was for something in one of the harbour-side northern suburbs, but in the end they settled on a flat in Marlborough Hall, Roslyn Avenue King's Cross. On one side the flat had a view of Rushcutters Bay, on the other, busy Macleay Street. Nothing could have been more of a contrast to the suburban tranquillity of St Ives, and they found the change invigorating. King's Cross was still the bohemian quarter of Sydney, sleazy around the edges, but with 'continental' delicatessens and greengrocers which had more exotic produce than could be found in suburban shops. There were also good restaurants and the Minerva Theatre around the corner, while the passing parade of 'foreigners' and eccentrics was a constant source of interest.

Flat life seemed to be a restorative for Mildred. A few weeks after they had moved in, she wrote that 'we still feel as though we are on a sort of holiday'. And indeed, the idea was also to explore parts of Sydney they were not familiar with. The public transport available at Kings Cross meant that Mildred was much more of a free agent than at St Ives where, not driving a car, she was dependent either on the poor bus service to Pymble station or a lift from Philip. And at Kings Cross it was easy to be lazy and get take-away food from down the street, something of a novelty in Australia then. On Philip's birthday they led a small family group down Macleay Street to the glitzy new Chevron Silver Spade ('subdued lighting and real candles on the table' Mildred noted) where they had a delicious three-course dinner while being entertained by the 'Gaslight Gaieties' music hall floor show. Afterwards they returned to the flat for a 'little birthday supper'.

They had, up to this time, had no difficulty in resisting the temptation of television, which had been introduced in Melbourne and Sydney in 1956. Now, as part of the mood of holiday permissiveness, they rented a set, so their letters now contained comments on the programs sampled. Mildred reported that Philip was 'quite interested, now that he hasn't the piano to practise on'.

Recovering from her recent bout of illness Mildred was back at the Julian Ashton Art School, which was just an easy bus trip away. While living in the flat she painted the view from the window overlooking Macleay Street. Through a gap between the tall 1930s blocks of flats the focus of the painting is the El Alamein Fountain, which had only recently been turned on, a ball of sparkling water effervescing in this densely built urban environment. A few figures scurry about their business. The painting has a charming, slightly naïf edge to it, emphasised by the view being from above; it must be one of the earliest representations in paint of the El Alamein Fountain, which quickly became almost as well known and appreciated as the Archibald Fountain in Hyde Park.

For a few months Mildred and Philip enjoyed Kings Cross to the full. Tucked away in their cosy flat they were alone together in a way that they had not been since the London years, when Barbara was away at school and I was in the care of a nanny. And, exploring this unfamiliar inner suburban territory at their Kings Cross doorstep, they might well have been reminded of their life when they were sharing the experience of discovering London.

And then in September Mildred fell ill again. At first it was just some niggling stomach pains; then she was having trouble keeping food down, and had the feeling of some sort of internal blockage; she thought she might have thrown something out of place lifting the sewing machine. An x-ray confirmed a blockage in the bowel. An operation was necessary. This identified the presence of cancer – at first the doctors refrained from using the actual word – though its extent was uncertain. At least the operation was able to relieve the discomfort caused by the blockage.

There was a long wait for the pathologist's report which, when it came, was not conclusive. It was thought it might have been an ovarian growth, in which case a hysterectomy was a possibility. But if there was to be a second operation the priority was for Mildred to regain her strength first. She had not been told of the emerging diagnosis. But one day she asked Philip if a growth might have been the cause of her illness. Sensibly, he replied that this was possible. She took this calmly. Later, when examined by a gynaecologist whom she liked, she asked point blank what was wrong with her and he confirmed the presence of a malignant growth. Again she received this news – which she already had reason to suspect – without fuss or apparent emotion. It was a great relief all round that there was now no need for the family to maintain the pretence of secrecy.

In late October Mildred was discharged from hospital. It now seemed to be a process of slow recovery, Mildred and Philip enjoying a few weeks staying with Barbara and John in their recently renovated Cammeray house, followed by a week or two at Terrigal before returning to the Kings Cross flat. Any thought of a second operation had apparently been put aside; doctors seemed to be deliberately vague about the outlook. But, in the midst of all the family concern – there had been a steady stream of visitors at the hospital, and both Philip and Barbara had found dealing with the many inquiring telephone calls a strain – there was a semblance of life returning to normal. And Mildred herself seemed not only calm but relaxed, determined to enjoy the things that mattered to her. She was soon back at the art school, and she and Philip resumed their usual program of concerts and plays.

The six months in Kings Cross had been extended to a year, but in mid 1962 Philip and Mildred returned to the house in St Ives. In August Philip turned sixty. Barbara and John hosted a dinner party for the celebration and it was a lively and happy occasion. At home Philip was busy painting one of the bedrooms which was going to serve as Mildred's studio. With its now white walls and the curtains taken down he reported that the room had 'a pretty good even light till the late afternoon'. There was a sense of guarded determination to live a normal life.

But in a letter to me Father added a PS that 'Frau keeps well despite periods of discomfort'.

In England I followed the news of my mother's illness with concern and indeed some anguish born of distance. But with her slow, partial recovery through the early months of 1962 there seemed no urgent need for my return. It was felt, too, that any sudden return on my part would give the impression that her condition had become critical.

In London Ron and I were struggling to survive, and I had managed to get some chorus work, including a gruelling six month stint in a London Palladium variety show starring Harry Secombe. In August 1962 I had a minor breakthrough in being cast in a Bristol Old Vic production of 'Fiorello', a current Broadway musical about New York's legendary mayor of the 1930s Fiorello H La Guardia. I was in Bristol rehearsing when the news from home grew more worrying. In a letter my mother made a passing reference to having 'a touch of jaundice'. Then in September came the grim estimate from doctors that she might have only two to three months. A few days after receiving this news 'Fiorello' opened to some acclaim in Bristol. Soon a transfer to the West End was being talked about.

I was by this time planning my return flight in communication with Father, who was going to have to lend me the money for the fare. Yet in a letter I received in mid-September my mother preserved the tone of normality, relating news about family and neighbours, and reporting on visits to the theatre to see the musical 'The Sentimental Bloke' and the touring Sadlers Wells production of Offenbach's 'Orpheus in the Underworld'. Only towards the end of the letter did she mention being very tired after having been out two nights running.

I played the first week of 'Fiorello' in London before leaving the production to fly home on 14 October. On the morning of the 16th I was back at 14 Benaroon Avenue. I learned on my arrival that my mother's decline over the last week or two had been rapid, so I was prepared for the gaunt, sallow face propped up on the pillows. 'I didn't think I'd make it,' she said ruefully, implying that, with my pending return, it had been a race against time. We chatted intermittently through the day. She asked me how much the airfare had cost. I realised later she was calculating whether my share of the small bequest she was leaving Barbara and me would cover it.

She was unable to eat anything now, but there was a commercial orange-flavoured sorbet which provided some refreshment. She said how nice it was, and with the little wooden spoon in her hand asked if I would I like a taste. I shook my head, saying we were about to sit down to the dinner which Barbara was cooking. Ever since I have regretted not accepting the offered sorbet.

While we were eating our grim dinner Frau, tended by the night nurse, was violently ill. When I went in to see her afterwards she was exhausted. Her eyes half closed, she lay back restlessly on the pillows; 'I just want to sleep', she said, as if sheer weariness had blotted out anything else she might have wanted to say.

I collapsed with jet lag into the bed in my old room. I was awakened in the early hours of the morning to be told that my mother – otherwise known as Pearl, Mildred or Frau – had just died.

Philip was proud that up to the very last night, when the nurse was called in, he had, as always, been sharing the double bed with Mildred. In one letter he mentioned that they had been unable to celebrate their 35th wedding anniversary on 1 October with the usual dinner out and show. But it was, in a sense, observed, and Philip's mistake in seeking to arrange the wedding for 31 September wryly remembered.

At some point in her dying, Mildred, reflecting on life and marriage, said to Barbara that she wondered whether she had been too hard on Philip when she found the letter from Clare. I assume she was thinking of that escape to Sydney with us, the children, in tow, which inevitably meant that news of the crisis spread around the family. Who knows what excuses he made in Dubbo for the sudden absence of the family, but it was humiliating for him. When the crisis had been resolved and family life resumed Philip was nevertheless aware of the silent disapproval of some of Mildred's relatives, particularly her mother Edith. He lived it down, and made a point of being generous to Edith, who lived with us for some years in the 1950s. He accepted without question the responsibilities that being a member of a family entailed in those days.

He and Mildred had worked hard to create a happy home after the troubles of war and had in large measure succeeded. Mildred was all too aware of Philip's faults – he had, indeed, confessed them to her, saying he wasn't worthy of her love. In their romantic courtship they had enjoyed the emotional intimacy of lovers, and Philip's later misdemeanours seemed like a betrayal and reinforced her natural reserve. She had been badly hurt. But there remained an important bond between them – and the memories of their time in England were part of that. That bond was particularly evident through her episodes of illness when he was loyal and caring. And their time in the Kings Cross flat recaptured something of the happiness of the early days of their marriage.

As the new day dawned on 17 October the three of us, the remaining members of the family unit, sat around the dining room table discussing the funeral arrangements. Although we had no theoretical objection to cremation, we agreed that we preferred the traditional form of burial. St John's Gordon, which had been part of our wartime memories, was just a mile or two from St Ives, and had a small picturesque graveyard; we discovered that, surprisingly, it had a vacant lot.

In 1962 the Book of Common Prayer still ruled the Church of England, so it was 'The Order for the Burial of the Dead'. One of its opening texts offers that grim, uncompromising reminder:

> We brought nothing into this world, and it is certain we can carry nothing out.

> The Lord gave, and the Lord hath taken away; blessed be the name of the Lord.

One of the hymns sung in the church was 'Blessed are the pure in heart' which we thought fitting.

When the service had come to its emotional close, we were standing around outside the church engaged in self-conscious funeral conversation, the pause before the family group would accompany the coffin down to the waiting grave for the burial, when a young man, a few inches shorter than me with ginger hair, approached me. He quietly introduced himself: it was Ronnie, the school playmate from my wartime years at Gordon Public School. We had not stayed in touch, but, as a parishioner of the local church, he must have learned about my mother's death and funeral. He remembered my mother; more particularly he remembered how, at the time of his own mother's death, when he was no more than eight, she had consoled him in his grief. I was moved that he had come, but at a loss for words. He was with his wife; they politely declined to join us for the later refreshments and withdrew. I was never to see him again.

Afterwards the coffin was lowered into the earth and the final prayers said. Barbara wrote the epitaph which was later inscribed on the stone:

Gentle, kind and well-beloved,
In life as death most brave.
May her quiet spirit
Approve this quiet grave.

Chapter 7

EPILOGUE

People do what they can; they were good people,
They cared for us and loved us. Once they stood
Tall in my childhood as the school, the steeple.
How can I judge without ingratitude?

— James McAuley

With Mildred's death Philip was on his own in the house at St Ives. He was lonely; he was a man who needed company and companionship. The year he and Mildred had spent in the Kings Cross flat had whetted his appetite for something different from the stereotypical 'house and garden' suburbia of 14 Benaroon Avenue. He had always had a hankering for something more cosmopolitan which was one reason he had enjoyed London so much.

Sydney was seeing the beginning of an interest in the regeneration of the inner suburbs, some of which had for years been dismissed as slums. Terrace houses, with their cast iron balconies, were attracting middle-class young couples who would set about renovating them. And while the inner suburbs had seen the building of numerous blocks of flats between the wars (like Marlborough Hall in Kings Cross) now architects were drawing up plans for much more ambitious development projects.

The trailblazer – and to this day still a controversial building – was Harry Seidler's Blues Point Tower, completed in 1961. Viennese-born Seidler, probably Sydney's best known modernist architect then, opened a practice in Sydney in 1949. The house he designed for his parents, known as the Rose Seidler House, caused a considerable stir with its clean lines and arresting severity. The 25-floor Blues Point Tower was the tallest residential building in Sydney; it also pioneered the introduction of strata title for an apartment building.

That this monumental pillar of apartments had been allowed on Blues Point, a finger of land on the northern side of the harbour which had been free of any high-rise development, angered some people. Was this what was going to happen to Sydney's harbour-side suburbs? (It was.) Its uncompromising exterior, with its unusual patterning of windows, also was a cause for offence. But the building soon had its supporters, and of course one of its attractions was that it offered spectacular views in all directions. There was also a ferry service, the wharf almost at the Tower's doorstep, which took you to Circular Quay in ten minutes.

In 1963 Philip rented a flat in the Tower; later, with the sale of 14 Benaroon Avenue, he bought one. In one direction you looked across to the great arch of the Bridge, hearing the rumble of trains crossing it, not to mention the distant screams of those enjoying the thrills of the big dipper at Luna Park at its feet: looking south across to Darling Harbour you witnessed the shipping traffic up and down the harbour, the larger ships coming close enough to be almost alarming at first sight. Philip took to the Blues Point Tower immediately.

Soon after the funeral I was out doing the theatrical rounds looking for work: I was, after all, penniless, and owing my father the air fare. I had the good fortune to be cast in the first Australian production of the Rodgers and Hammerstein musical 'The King and I', playing what used to be called the juvenile lead, one of the tragic young lovers who dies in Act 2 (offstage, a cause for regret on my part). I was to spend the next eighteen months touring Australia and New Zealand with the show. This long separation from Ron had its effect on both of us; as the prospects for my career seemed better here than in England we drifted apart and, though staying in touch and remaining friends, eventually both entered new relationships.

After its Melbourne season 'The King and I' moved to Sydney in mid-1963 where I stayed with my father in his apartment in the Tower. Coming home late after the nightly show I would often find he had retired; in the morning he would usually be off to Jones & Rickard before I arose.

One day, in the apartment on my own, I – even now, almost fifty years later, I shrink a little from this confession – wandered into my father's bedroom. I don't think I can even claim the excuse of doing some housework, vacuuming or dusting. Looking at his bedside table I felt a tingle of curiosity. Barbara and I were soon aware after our mother's death that Father was seeking female company, and that the possibility of future marriage was likely to be something on his mind. We felt for him and his need for companionship, but we were sometimes amused by the careful preliminaries of courtship, and his coyness, to us, about his intentions. What was I imagining I might find in his bedside drawer? Some clue, perhaps, to the private self that had been hidden from us?

What I found might indeed be seen as just that – but back then it came as a total shock. It was a carbon copy of a typed aerogram letter to Clare, written soon after Mildred's death. Clare! Those childhood memories from my sleep-out in Dubbo came flooding back. It was, essentially, a proposal of marriage. He reflected on the sadness of Mildred's death, but made a point of noting that she had, in those last painful days, told him she wanted him to be happy. 'I knew what she meant Clare.' In other words he understood Mildred to have given him permission to renew, all these years later, the relationship with Clare. It was a warm, even passionate letter, full of hope for the future, assuming somehow that they could simply pick up the relationship where they had left off.

Tucked underneath it was Clare's handwritten reply. Yes, she had such happy memories of their brief time together; there was a reference to his 'big brown arms' embracing her. But it was too late for what Philip was asking her to do. In her late fifties she was daunted by the prospect of being uprooted from her life in England and moving to Australia. Leaving England would also mean separation from her children, now grown up, and their lives. It was with sincere regret that she felt compelled to decline Philip's proposal.

Interested as I was to read these letters I was also overcome with some guilt at my snooping in my father's bedside table. Indeed, I was so ashamed at what I had done that I told no one about my discovery, not even Barbara. Actually, I am not sure that I read the letters in their entirety: I have a memory of quickly perusing them and having absorbed the gist of their content hastily returning them to the drawer. I had not taken proper note of Clare's full name and address. She was just 'Clare'.

As a biographer and historian I was later to regret that I didn't take careful notes. If only there had been a photocopier handy! (Such machines hardly existed then.) Indeed it was some time before I even referred to the discovery in my journal, which was, in the 1960s, intermittent at the best of times. It was my secret, and to even put it into words on paper seemed somehow a betrayal of my father.

Now I can put this exchange of letters into some context. Clare's husband Trevor had died in 1958. Although not appearing to have been brought up a Catholic, Trevor was buried with Roman Catholic rites, so at some point he must have 'turned', as going over to Rome was sometimes described then. Clare may have separated from Trevor before his death but they were unlikely to have divorced because of his Catholicism. It is clear that Philip knew that Trevor had died and that Clare was free to marry him when he wrote the letter to her. So they must have stayed in touch over the years: when Philip was in Dubbo she had written to him at the Stores Depot, and in Sydney she could have written care of Jones & Rickard. Indeed when Philip said 'I knew what she meant Clare' it even throws up the possibility that Mildred was aware of the change in Clare's status. At the very least it suggests that Mildred knew that Clare had remained important to him.

Their intermittent correspondence over the years must have convinced Philip that there was still a strong attachment between them, otherwise he would hardly have presumed to write proposing marriage. But one might hazard that, apart from the reasons she gave him, for Clare the sense conveyed by Philip of Mildred from the grave 'permitting' their marriage may not have been enticing. Why, she might have been tempted to ask, should that be necessary? And how would her arrival in Australia be explained? Who in the family she would be joining might know the history of their affair?

There is something engaging about Philip's optimistic belief that twenty years later he and Clare could so easily pick up the threads of their whirlwind war romance. One wonders if they had spoken on the phone at all. International phone calls, with their time constraints, were often nervous, self-conscious exchanges, and it is understandable that he thought that for what he was proposing a letter was required. At the same time I am struck by the fact that his letter is *typed*; my father's letters to me were almost without exception handwritten. But in this case he wanted to have a carbon copy; he wanted to have a record of precisely what he had said in this crucial message.

The mystery of Clare remains. We have only hints of what she must have been like from Philip, and from my memory of the exchange of letters between them that I discovered in his bedside drawer all those years ago. And yet she is not faceless. There is still that small, smiling photograph of the woman with her little girl in a London garden, the photograph that Mildred carefully inserted in the shoebox of Philip's wartime letters.

In 1965 Philip married Pam, a friend of our cousin Pauline. Pam was 37 and had recently been appointed to a lectureship in biochemistry at the

University of New South Wales, the beginning of a new career for her. She had left school at the Intermediate Certificate and completed a secretarial course, getting a job in the library of the Sydney *Daily Telegraph*, where her father was a journalist. Having studied at night for matriculation at TAFE, at 25 she won a mature-age scholarship and enrolled in science at Sydney University, setting forth on the long academic haul culminating in a PhD at London University. It was still then the normal expectation for graduates to gravitate to England to study for their doctorates. Pam would never have regarded herself as a feminist in the political sense, but her career was a striking example of the determination required of women if they were to succeed in academia, which in the 1950s was still predominantly a man's world. She would go on to gain a chair and become the head of the newly created School of Biological Technologies at New South Wales University. Philip always took an interest in her career and was proud of her achievements. They lived in the Blues Point Tower unit for some time before moving back to suburbia, a house in East Lindfield, not so very far from St Ives.

Pam also wanted to have children. Philip was more than happy to go along with that. He told Pam he would have liked to have had four children; he didn't elaborate, but one might assume that Mildred's health was a factor in preventing that. Sadly, Pam had a miscarriage and the new family never eventuated.

For whatever reason Philip had not kept Mildred's wartime letters to him. But the shoebox of his letters, which Mildred had preserved, passed into his hands on her death. He made no attempt to cull them, as he might have been tempted to do: the letters relating to the woman in the red coat, which hardly reflect well on him, survive. Did he ever revisit his letters? If he had he would have come across that little slip of paper recording Clare's name and address together with the tiny photograph which Mildred had inserted. It is possible, of course, that he couldn't bring himself to reread his letters because they were, in a sense, an exercise in deception, a record of what he was not telling her – his falling in love with Clare.

Nevertheless he kept them. Perhaps he wanted Barbara and I to read them, to bare his soul before us (including that last abject letter from Dubbo asking Mildred to come home) in a way that he could never do face to face. He was an emotional man, and there were times when I sensed that he felt we had, as children, sat in silent judgment on him, and, however affectionate we were towards him, that we had retained something of that moral reproach. I sometimes wished I had been able to ask him about Clare, but I don't know how he would have handled it; at the very least I think he would have been deeply embarrassed.

Philip had ten happy years with Pam, before suffering a stroke in 1975. He made a partial recovery, but it was not an easy time for either of them. Two days before Christmas 1977 he and Pam had just returned from a party at neighbours' across the street when in the kitchen at about 10.30pm Philip collapsed in mid sentence and died.

I had come up from Melbourne that morning on the annual Christmas pilgrimage and was staying with Barbara and John; I had spoken to my father earlier in the evening. When Pam rang with the news John drove me up to East Lindfield. As it happened the neighbourhood couple Philip and Pam had been visiting were both doctors and they had been able to confirm the death. When John and I arrived it was agreed that the three of us were in need of a whisky, and I had the surreal experience of going into the kitchen, observing my father's body on the floor, and stepping over him (though of course that corpse was no longer 'him') to get some water from the tap.

That night the funeral director was rung and it must have been close to midnight when the hearse slid discreetly down the street; a young man with long blond hair, who had clearly climbed into the compulsory suit with some haste, arrived on the doorstep. There were the practicalities to be dealt with: the removal of Father's watch, pockets searched for keys and wallet. Another man materialised and finally a stretcher bearing what was now only a shape was carried to the front door and down to the hearse, which disappeared quietly into the night.

I stayed with Pam for the next few days. Christmas was not a good time to be arranging a funeral. We were agreed that Father would have preferred burial, and it was Pam's suggestion that he should be buried with our mother. A stonemason had to be engaged to lift the slab so that the grave could be opened. His services were secured but the gravedigger was a problem. He was on holidays and there was some difficulty contacting him; he reluctantly consented but, as he had some distance to travel requested that the funeral be no later than one o'clock. It was set for 28 December. And first of all, of course, there was the family Christmas at Barbara and John's to contend with, which could hardly be cancelled.

On one of these intervening days Pam engaged me in a heart-to-heart. 'There were no secrets between your father and me,' she said. Before they were married Father told her about Clare. Although he was shy about raising the subject – and they were never to talk about it again – he felt the need to make clear the importance of Clare in their life. They had met through music and had fallen in love. After his return to Australia they had stayed in touch but this, he made clear, had now ceased.

I was moved that Pam felt the need to tell me this, as if she were defending Philip to his children; it confirmed my feeling that to the extent that Barbara and I had been involved in that brief separation, when our mother took us down to Sydney, he had seen us as being arrayed against him. Pam said that Philip was a highly sexed man; indeed, the stroke had by no means put an end to their sex life. Prostitutes were not in his line; in England he needed a relationship, though perhaps with Clare he got more than he had bargained for. It was possible, Pam believed, to be in love with two people at the same time.

Although Father had told Pam about Clare, there was one confession he did not feel able to make – that he had proposed to Clare after our mother's death. And of course there was no point in my telling her. It occurred to me that there was also a practical motive for Father making Pam aware of his wartime affair. He knew members of the wider family had long memories and that Pam might hear of his infidelity from them. Telling her was a sensible precaution. And so it proved: one relative took Pam aside to whisper the story of the affair, and she had the satisfaction of saying she already knew about it.

Returning to St John's Gordon for Father's funeral inevitably revived memories of that other funeral, fifteen years earlier. Emerging from the church into the sunlight we moved down the slope to the open grave where I could see the gravedigger waiting for us. When we had assembled and the coffin had been placed in position I became aware of a macabre difficulty: the coffin was not going to fit into the open grave. My fears were confirmed by a whispered conference between the master of ceremonies and the clergy. The master of ceremonies then approached Pam and myself and said that as the coffin would have to be tipped in rather than lowered they would leave that till after the ceremony. Later, with the grave closed and the stone slab returned to its position the inscription for Philip Magnus Rickard would be added with the epigraph, 'A strong spirit and a tender heart'.

So, in death, Philip and Mildred were reunited, even if there was that problem, which might almost have seemed symbolic, in adapting the grave to receive his coffin. It was fifty years since their wedding and that romantic time when young Philip arrived on Mildred's doorstep bearing his Sunday gift, a basket of freshly picked nectarines.

Fifty years later Australia had changed, the Empire had disintegrated, the world was a different place. The institution of marriage had also changed. Whatever Philip's faults were, he shared with Mildred an understanding of marriage, with its rules, both written and unwritten, which by 1977 was going out of fashion. When they walked down the aisle in 1927 to begin their life together they had a clear idea of the commitment they were making and the responsibilities they were accepting. When the crisis in their marriage erupted they felt, in the end, bound by that commitment. For some couples, in similar situations, the result would have been an unhappy household, poisoned by a legacy of hostility and bitterness. But Philip and Mildred were able to recover enough of a loving relationship to reconstitute and sustain a happy family home.

Acknowledging the warning in McAuley's poem, I shrink from judging my parents. But I am glad to say that, yes,

they were good people,
They cared for us and loved us.